D0053103

COURAGEOUS

Gentleness

FOLLOWING CHRIST'S EXAMPLE OF RESTRAINED STRENGTH

MARY ANN FROEHLICH

DISCOVERY HOUSE

P U B L I S H E R S®

Feeding the Soul with the Word of God

Courageous Gentleness: Following Christ's Example of Restrained Strength

Discovery House is affiliated with RBC Ministries, Grand Rapids, Michigan.

Requests for permission to quote from this book should be directed to: Permissions Department, Discovery House Publishers, P.O. Box 3566, Grand Rapids, MI 49501, or contact us by e-mail at permissionsdept@dhp.org

Interior designed by Melissa Elenbaas

ISBN 978-1-57293-819-9

Printed in the United States of America

First printing in 2014

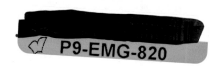
To my gentle Lord
and my friends and family
who have tenderly extended
His soothing embrace.

CONTENTS

Acknowledgments

Many thanks to:

My friends at Discovery House, who encourage my writing ministry and masterfully guide my book projects to fruition.

My husband, John, for his unconditional love, generous laughter, and tangible support through many years of writing.

My family, who is the anchor and joy of my life.

Dan Wolke for sharing his ministry of gentleness and compassion with readers.

Other contributors who shared their ministries but chose to remain anonymous.

All my dear friends, who have modeled Christ's gentleness and kindness through a lifetime of friendship.

Is Gentleness for Wimps?

*R*ecently I attended a memorial service for Wilma, a ninety-year-old saint who was known for her deep faith, kindness, and gentle spirit. I had listened through the years to Wilma's children, daughter-in-law, grandchildren, nieces, nephews, friends, and other family members proclaim how gentle she was, emphasizing that she had never made one critical, unkind comment to them. Coming from a family where members speak their minds and never sugarcoat the truth, I marveled at these statements.

During the eulogy, the pastor of Wilma's church expounded on examples of her gentleness and concluded, "In spite of Wilma's quiet and gentle spirit, she impacted everyone around her for Jesus Christ."

In spite of?

Something is eerily amiss today. This pastor's perspective gives us an honest glimpse into an unspoken belief held by many Christians steeped in American culture. We already know that our culture does not prize a gentle, quiet spirit. We are taught to stand up for ourselves and not be taken advantage of. We are respected for bulldozing through obstacles and challenges in pursuit of our goals. We learn early in life that the squeaky wheel gets oiled. We would not readily admit it but daily practicing a quiet, humble, gentle spirit is not top priority on our list of qualities we pursue to make a godly difference in this world in the name of Jesus Christ.

We want to be people of action, going boldly into the world to preach the good news, speaking the truth, standing up for what's right, and fighting the enemy of our soul. This emphasis embodies our American pioneer spirit. We often equate following God with *going*. Christian stores sell books about revolutionary faith, warrior faith, revolutionary parenting, and revolutionary churches. We are inspired by the image of participating in a revolution or fighting the good fight on life's battlefield.

We want to be soldiers or warriors for God. Ephesians 6:10–17 inspires us to put on the full armor of God to fight our spiritual enemy: "For our struggle is not against flesh and blood, but against the rulers, against the authorities, against the powers of this dark world and against the spiritual forces of evil in the heavenly realms" (v. 12). We gravitate to the military imagery of fighting and stories about soldiers in biblical times. We are at war. We want to be filled with the strength and power of the God of the universe and His Son, who defeated death for eternity. We want to change the world in the name of Jesus Christ. This is exciting stuff!

But the idea of having a quiet, humble, and gentle spirit? That sounds weak, passive, and . . . a little wimpy. That sounds like holding back, not marching forward. That sounds like holding our tongue, not speaking out. But here is the countercultural rub. Scripture teaches us that those qualities are the most powerful, transformative way to mirror Jesus Christ to a hurting world. The love of Christ is a weapon of unmatched power. Romans 13:14 tells us to be clothed in Jesus Christ. Colossians 3:12 tells us what this new wardrobe looks like: "As God's chosen people, holy and dearly loved, clothe yourselves with compassion, kindness, humility, gentleness and patience."

Yes, we do put on our armor to battle the spiritual forces of evil. But we also must don the clothing of Christ to tenderly love hurting people in a broken world. We may feel emboldened by Paul's words, "Be on your guard; stand firm in the faith; be courageous; be strong" (1 Corinthians 6:13), but we must not forget that the next verse says this: "Do everything in love." Everything? Yes, everything. Courage and strength immersed in God's love should lead to life-altering shifts in all our relationships, from interacting with strangers to dealing with our closest family members.

In this book we will study the tangible face of Christ's love expressed through gentleness. In the first section we will take a scriptural journey to define biblical gentleness, which is radically different from the word's view of gentleness. Then we will ask the hard question, "Are Christians known for their gentleness today?" In our second section, we will learn ways to practice Christ's gentleness in the trenches of daily life.

We will see that Wilma daily pointed the way to Jesus Christ throughout her life *because* she practiced a quiet, gentle, and loving spirit—not in spite of it. And God calls us to do the same. Make no mistake about it. This is the toughest calling. Is gentleness for wimps? Quite the opposite! Gentleness is the response of Christ's strongest and most courageous followers.

Your beauty should not come from outward adornment, such as elaborate hairstyles and the wearing of gold jewelry and fine clothes. Rather, it should be that of your inner self, the unfading beauty of a gentle and quiet spirit, which is of great worth in God's sight.

1 Peter 3:3–4

The Holy Spirit is the most perfect gift of the Father to men, and yet He is the one gift the Father gives most easily.

—Thomas Merton

The eternal and ultimate purpose of God by his Spirit is to make us like Christ.

—John Stott

If you are not in harmony with the Spirit, there is no enemy who is worse or more troublesome to the soul than you yourself.

—Thomas à Kempis

WHAT IS BIBLICAL GENTLENESS?

Gentleness is never a cowardly retreat from reality.
—Stanley Horton

*A*s I sat waiting with my family in a hospital wing during my father's open heart surgery, we overheard doctors tell other families the surgery outcomes of their loved ones. One family's surgeon was brutally blunt, "The surgery didn't work. Your husband is dying. There's nothing I could do." Then he quickly left.

A few minutes later our surgeon brought us the same news. My father barely survived the surgery. If he lived, he could be paralyzed. He would probably die. Our doctor gently told us this bad news with compassion, and he spent time consoling us. My father died within forty-eight hours. But we were grateful to have a kind and gentle physician caring for us.

The gentleness our doctor portrayed is not weakness. It is not cowardice. Gentleness is a conscious decision to temper one's knowledge, skills, authority, or power with kindness and compassion. Gentleness does not refer to *what* we do but *how* we do it. Gentleness does not refer to *what* we know but *how* we share that knowledge.

If your experiences have been similar to mine, you have been instructed by gentle teachers as well as harsh, impatient ones. You have been trained by gentle coaches as well as cruel ones who humiliate students. You have been treated by gentle, compassionate doctors and nurses as well as rushed ones who do not handle instruments gently as they examine you. You have been employed by gentle, kind bosses who lead by example as well as angry, critical ones. Your parents may have disciplined you with gentleness but other times in anger. You may have attended churches with gentle pastors as well as severe ones.

I think of Mr. Wilson, my high school physical education teacher. Because I was promoted past a grade in elementary school, I was always younger and smaller than my peers—with zero athletic ability. Mr. Wilson was the first physical education teacher who kindly and gently helped me improve. He was a true educator. He never became angry or frustrated with his less capable students. His patience never waned as he taught us skills that were natural for athletic students but foreign to the rest of us. He always encouraged us and never humiliated us.

One day a friend invited me to an after-school Bible study in a neighbor's home. I agreed to go because I was exploring Christianity. When I arrived, I was surprised to discover that Mr. Wilson led the study. Suddenly, his gentle approach made perfect sense. I didn't need to know that Mr. Wilson followed Christ to observe that he was remarkably different.

Can most Christians claim a similar gentle reputation? Throughout life you have probably formed your own definitions of gentleness. Think about how your experiences with gentle or ungentle people have affected you. Next we will look at how God's Word defines gentleness.

GENTLENESS AND MEEKNESS

The closest translation of the word *gentleness* is *meekness*. If our culture has a negative response to gentleness, associating it with weakness, it is downright offended by the word *meekness*. Would you have purchased a book entitled *Practicing Meekness* or *How to Be More Meek and Mild*?

Meek can be defined as "gentle, quiet, and submissive," while *mild* is defined as "gentle, not easily provoked." The Old English form of *mild* is *milde*, which means "gracious." Gracious is not only defined as being courteous and kind but as showing God's divine grace. Do these definitions communicate submissive, weak meekness? Paul assures us that they should not: "For the Spirit God gave us does not make us timid, but gives us a spirit of power, love and self-discipline" (2 Timothy 1:7).

Doesn't a meek person sound like a gentle, timid, and quiet one? It does to me. Yet Scripture describes a meek person as gentle and quiet, filled with a spirit of power, love, and self-discipline, but with not one hint of timidity or fear.

God's Word describes a meek, gentle powerhouse. Practicing gentleness in our culture requires quiet, determined strength and unflinching boldness. Indeed, showing gentleness is a courageous act.

In 2 Corinthians 10:1 (NKJV) Paul appeals to the church at Corinth by "meekness" (*prautes*) and "gentleness" (*epieikeias*) of Christ. These two Greek words, *prautes* and *epieikeias*, are used throughout the New Testament to describe gentleness and meekness. Theologian Stanley Horton says that the best translation of *gentleness* in our current English language is *kindness*.[1] The King James Version translates the Greek word *chrestotes* as "gentleness" in Galatians 5:22 but translates it as "kindness" in other passages.

Note our Lord's words in the Sermon on the Mount using *prautes*: "Blessed are the meek, for they will inherit the earth" (Matthew 5:5). This is the most common translation. Here are other versions, substituting "gentleness" for "meekness":

- "Blessed are the gentle, for they shall inherit the earth" (NASB).
- "How blest are those of a gentle spirit; they shall have the earth for their possession" (NEB).

Several verses in the New Testament translate *prautes* as "humility." This fits with the Old Testament references to meekness. *Anav* is the Hebrew word for "meekness." It also refers to being lowly, poor, and humble. For example, *anav* means "humble" in Zephaniah 2:3 (TJB): "Seek Yahweh, all you, the humble of the earth, who obey his commands. Seek integrity, seek humility."

Anavah is translated as "meekness, humility, or gentleness." Now you can understand why the King James Version describes Moses in Numbers 12:3 as the meekest man on earth while some other translations describe him as the most humble man on earth.

Horton writes, "Meekness is not a self-debasing or a belittling of oneself. Rather it is a true humility that does not consider itself too good to do the humble tasks. It is not too big or self-important to be courteous, considerate, and gentle with everyone."[2]

THE SCOPE OF GENTLENESS

You are probably beginning to recognize the scope of the word *gentleness* and its translations (meekness, humility, kindness) as used in Scripture. When I spoke with different people about the topic of this book, most responded, "Gentleness? So your book is about *that* fruit of the Spirit." We tend to compartmentalize it. We relegate it to a list. This is one reason why practicing gentleness is sometimes misunderstood. Gentleness may be the fruit of the spirit, but you can see from the previous section that its biblical importance is much broader than that topic.

In Galatians 3:27, Paul tells us that we are clothed in Christ. We are *covered* with Christ. Review the clothing Paul calls us to wear in Colossians:

> Therefore, as God's chosen people, holy and dearly loved, clothe yourselves with *compassion, kindness, humility, gentleness and patience.* Bear with each other and forgive one another if any of you has a grievance against someone. Forgive as the Lord forgave you. And over all these virtues put on love, which binds them all together in perfect unity. Let the *peace* of Christ rule in your hearts, since as members of one body you were called to peace.
>
> Colossians 3:12–15

Now compare the clothing of Christ with the fruit of the Spirit:

> But the fruit of the Spirit is *love, joy, peace, patience, kindness, goodness, faithfulness, gentleness* and *self-control.* Against such things there is no law. Those who belong to Christ Jesus have crucified the sinful nature with its passions and desires. Since we live by the Spirit, let us keep in step with the Spirit.
>
> Galatians 5:22–25 (NIV 1984)

Does Christ's clothing and spiritual fruit look similar? We note in both these passages that the traits come in one package. Throughout Scripture gentleness is always linked to other related Christlike qualities. Think of them as the facets of one stone. Gemstones have facets cut into them to optimize the stones, allowing them to reflect light. It is a complex process of cutting, grinding, and polishing—transforming the stone into a jewel. Imagine the Holy Spirit as the grinder and polisher of your spiritual facets, reflecting the light of Jesus Christ to the world. Jesus is the Perfecter of our faith (Hebrews 12:2).

GENTLENESS IS HEALTHY FRUIT

The fruit of the Spirit needs our cooperation for its development.

—Stanley Horton

The terms *gentle* and *gentleness*, which are mentioned throughout the Bible, remain a critical anchor of healthy spiritual fruit. I would suggest that *gentleness* is not simply a quality, trait, behavior, or characteristic. It is a *choice*.

The most helpful way to think about gentleness as fruit of the Spirit is to first realize what spiritual fruit is not.

Spiritual fruit is not plural. God intends for us to harvest healthy fruit, not fruits. The fruit of God's Holy Spirit is singular. It's an all-or-nothing experience. We do not pick and choose from the fruit of the Spirit listed in Galatians 5:22–23 like a breakfast buffet.

"Today's specials are love and peace. Tomorrow you can order patience."

If we are following Jesus, we desire to daily exhibit *all* the fruit of the Spirit. Remember that it comes as one package. Our fruit is evidence of our relationship with Jesus.

If we were on trial in a courtroom for following Jesus, our fruit would be the evidence that convicts us. It should make perfect sense that a gentle, kind, and loving person is also humble, patient, peaceful, and self-controlled. What should *not* make sense is when people separate these behaviors. For example, imagine a person who presents himself as kind and gentle in situations where there is no conflict. But when he is opposed, he becomes impatient and loses his temper. His demonstration of spiritual fruit is only a convenient act.

Spiritual fruit is not a personality trait. Sometimes we confuse people's temperaments and personality traits with spiritual fruit. "Monica is joyful. Eric is disciplined and self-controlled. Kristin is a quiet, gentle soul. Lisa has the gift of patience." Or we excuse our own lack of spiritual fruit by dismissing the "wimpy, less exciting" fruit. "I'm a Type A, driven person. I'm not passive. I don't hold back. That's just how God made me." No matter our natural bent and personality, we are each called to reflect Jesus and be gentle, patient, kind, peaceful, compassionate, humble, and self-controlled.

Spiritual fruit is not a spiritual gift. We do not receive spiritual fruit like we receive spiritual gifts to build up the body and further the kingdom of God (Romans 12:6–8). Christians receive different spiritual gifts: prophecy, service, teaching, encouragement, generosity, leadership, or mercy. God equips each of His children for a specific purpose. Yet our spiritual fruit guides *how* we share our spiritual gifts. An arrogant, harsh, impatient, or quick-tempered teacher or leader who claims to follow Christ does more harm than good.

Spiritual fruit does not automatically or easily appear. Fully ripened fruit of the Spirit does not automatically appear when we become followers of Jesus Christ. Fruit is grown and attentively tended over time. This process requires effort. The fruit of the Spirit must be practiced, developed, and harvested. The need for daily practice is so important that we will fully discuss it in chapter seven. Our spiritual gifts should certainly be developed and honed to honor God too. But spiritual maturity is our privileged life mission as we long to become more like our Lord.

Spiritual fruit is a single entity. It is not dependent on our natural temperament or personality. It should not be confused with our spiritual gifts. The process of developing healthy fruit requires plain hard work, fraught with challenges, as we rely on the Holy Spirit to guide us, help us, and comfort us.

> The Spirit will not remove all disappointment with God. The very titles given to the Spirit— Intercessor, Helper, Counselor, Comforter— imply there will be problems.
>
> —Philip Yancey

RIPENED FRUIT

Pure and simple, how we treat other people reveals our fruit. We long to become perfectly ripened fruit that tastes good to the world. Being gentle and kind are intangible ideals until we relate to someone in the flesh, especially someone who irritates or exasperates us.

Psalm 1:1–3 tells us: "Blessed is the one who does not walk in step with the wicked or stand in the way that sinners take or sit in the company of mockers, but who delight in the law of the Lord, and who meditate on his law day and night. That person is like a tree planted by streams of water, which yields its fruit in season and whose leaf does not wither—whatever they do prospers."

When we follow God, we are like a tree planted by streams of water. We yield healthy fruit and prosper. With our every thought and behavior, we want to resemble our Lord. Jesus tells us in John 15:5: "I am the vine; you are the branches. If you remain in me and I in you, you will bear much fruit; apart from me you can do nothing."

As we close this chapter, let's review the Christlike qualities that are viewed as synonyms for gentleness or mentioned in connection with gentleness. Gentle behavior is kind, humble, patient, peaceful, loving, compassionate, and self-controlled. Whether you think of these qualities as spiritual fruit or Christ's clothing, always remember that they are inseparable. You cannot practice one quality absent another. *We will bear much fruit if He is in us. We can do nothing apart from Him.*

Matthew 7:20 says that we will be recognized by our fruit. We may deceive ourselves into thinking that inconsistent actions are normal, but we cannot deceive God or the world He is determined to love through us.

But the wisdom that comes from heaven is first of all pure; then peace-loving, considerate, submissive, full of mercy and good fruit, impartial and sincere.

James 3:17

Personal Retreat

- Have you equated gentleness or meekness with weakness or strength?

- How do your experiences with gentleness or a lack of gentleness compare with scriptural definitions of gentleness?

- Mull over the thought that gentleness dictates *how* we share the love of Christ. Can you think of a time when you were more concerned about what information you shared rather than how you shared it?

- Did you have any common misperceptions about spiritual fruit?

- Think about how gentleness and related spiritual traits come in one package. What parts of the package do you find most challenging to practice?

- Think about how you can mirror Christ to the people in your world by being a gentle, meek powerhouse. Do you feel timid or bold?

God sometimes does His work with gentle drizzle, not storm.

—John Newton

Jesus loves us even when we are unlovable. The Good Shepherd has patiently searched for his wayward sheep. We have been honored by a divine gentleness and reverence that is beyond comprehension. Having experienced this tenderness, how can we not care deeply about civility?

—Richard Mouw

If there be in front of us any painful duty, strengthen us with the grace of courage; if any act of mercy, teach us tenderness and patience.

—Robert Louis Stevenson

2

IS GOD GENTLE?

As tenderly as a father treats his children, so Yahweh treats those who fear him; he knows what we are made of, he remembers we are dust.
                                              Psalm 103:13–14 TJB

*H*ave you ever had the privilege of watching a giant of a man hold his newborn child for the first time? He gently cradles his new son or daughter with such tenderness, love, and adoration that it can bring tears to our eyes. He could easily crush his newborn. Instead, He would die to protect his child. This father restrains his strength because he knows how helpless his child is. This is how God loves us. We have a tenderhearted heavenly Father.

Gentleness is a harness, hinged on controlled, disciplined strength. Jesus' life on earth was the epitome of restrained strength, which we will explore in the next chapter. A spirit of gentleness is embedded in the gospel message.

We have an all-powerful yet gentle God who could have destroyed us but instead chose to love us. In Genesis 32:22–31 we observe that God literally restrains himself as he wrestles with Jacob all through the night. Jacob says, "I have seen God face to face and my life is spared" (Genesis 32:31 NEB). This event is a microcosm of God's wrestling with His people throughout the Old Testament, repeatedly offering mercy instead of destruction.

Our Tender God in the Psalms

> Remember, Lord, thy tender care and thy love unfailing, shown from ages past.
>
> Psalms 25:6 NEB

> He rescues me from the pit of death and surrounds me with constant love, with tender affection; he contents me with all good in the prime of life, and my youth is ever new like an eagle's.
>
> Psalm 103:4–5 NEB

The stereotype of the angry, harsh God of the Old Testament versus the loving, merciful God of the New Testament confounds us. The assumed contrast between the God of the Law in the Old Testament and the God who came as a Savior in the New Testament clouds our understanding of the tender God described in the Psalms. Jesus was the culmination of God's tender mercy. God's gentleness is described as tenderness in the Old Testament, which usually includes restraint.

The Psalms show us that God is tender with us in three main ways:

1. God's tenderness rescues us from our brokenness. He wipes away our faults and washes away our sin. This is the ultimate act of gentle kindness.

> Have mercy on me, O God, in your goodness, in your great tenderness wipe away my faults; wash me clean of my guilt, purify me from my sin.
>
> Psalm 51:1–2 TJB

Yahweh is righteous and merciful, our God is tender-hearted; Yahweh defends the simple, he saved me when I was brought to my knees.

Psalm 116:5–6 TJB

In your loving kindness, answer me, Yahweh, in your great tenderness turn to me; do not hide your face from your servant, quick, I am in trouble, answer me; come to my side, redeem me, from so many enemies ransom me.

Psalm 69:16–18 TJB

2. God's tenderness shields us from His righteous anger. As a loving parent, He repeatedly restrains his anger. Because He created us, God compassionately understands how fragile His children are. He remembers that we are only dust. He treats us with painstaking gentleness.

Lord God, you who are always merciful and tender-hearted, slow to anger, always loving, always loyal, turn to me and pity me.

Psalm 86:15–16 TJB

Compassionately, however, he forgave their guilt instead of killing them, repeatedly repressing his anger instead of rousing his full wrath, remembering they were creatures of flesh, a puff of wind that passes and does not return.

Psalm 78:38–39 TJB

As tenderly as a father treats his children, so Yahweh treats those who fear him; he knows what we are made of, he remembers we are dust.

Psalm 103:13–14 TJB

3. God's tenderness assures that we are never treated as we deserve. This is the definition of mercy.

Yahweh is tender and compassionate, slow to anger, most loving; his indignation does not last for ever, his resentment exists a short time only; he never treats us, never punishes us, as our guilt and our sins deserve.

Psalm 103:8–10 TJB

If we truly understand that we are called to treat others as tenderly as God treats us, we will

- generously extend forgiveness and unconditional love to the unlovable.
- repeatedly restrain our anger and control our temper when we feel provoked.
- have compassion on others, realizing that they are as fragile and broken as we are.
- be tenderhearted and merciful, never treating others as we think they deserve.

The tenderness described above calls us to restrain our hurtful actions and thoughts in all our relationships, especially with difficult people. But what if God asks us to passionately love and pursue the most difficult and unlovable people in our lives? Isn't that asking too much? Did God ask too much of Hosea?

GO MARRY A WHORE

We are in danger of being stern where God is tender, and of being tender where God is stern.

—Oswald Chambers

If you have any doubts about God's limitless tender mercy and restraint, read the book of Hosea. Yahweh tells Hosea, "Go, marry a whore, and get children with a whore, for the country itself has become nothing but a whore by abandoning Yahweh" (Hosea 1:2 TJB).

Imagine that one of your close friends married a prostitute. They now have children together. A family has been formed. Your friend's decision to marry seemed like poor judgment (you said he was crazy) but he went ahead. Perhaps you were wrong to worry. But now your friend's spouse has returned to her former life, sleeping with other men and treating your friend like garbage. You are sure now that your friend will file for divorce and finally end this toxic relationship. Instead, your friend is doing everything possible to court his wife and repair their relationship. No matter her unfaithfulness, your friend remains faithful. In this same situation, God tells Hosea to take back his adulterous wife for the second time (Hosea 3:1).

Hosea is called to passionately pursue his undeserving wife as a mirror of the way God pursues His unfaithful people who worship other gods. We deceive ourselves if we think that we do not follow in the Israelites' footsteps. We also abandon God to worship a myriad of other gods—fame, prestige, wealth, material objects, lust, and other idols.

When you realize that *you* are the prostitute that God is pursuing and blocking all paths to protect (Hosea 2:6), you can hear the tenderness in His voice. He will go to any lengths to pursue you and woo you back to Him.

> But I will court her again and bring her into the wilderness, and I will speak to her tenderly there. There I will give back her vineyards to her and transform her Valley of Troubles into a Door of Hope.
>
> Hosea 2:14–15 TLB

> I will betroth you to myself forever, betroth you with integrity and justice, with tenderness and love; I will betroth you to myself with faithfulness, and you will come to know Yahweh.
>
> Hosea 2:21–22 TJB

DEFINITION OF A TENDER MAN

> Kept safe by virtue, he is ever steadfast, and leaves an imperishable memory behind him.
>
> Psalm 112:6 TJB

Psalm 112:4 defines the man who follows God as one who "shines like a lamp in the dark, he is merciful, tenderhearted, virtuous" (TJB). The man who follows God is tenderhearted and merciful. He is rock solid, unwavering in his faithfulness. His virtuous path keeps him safe. His behavior has an impact on the world, leaving an imperishable memory and legacy. This is the image of God that we are called to share with the world around us. This is the tender father described in the Psalms and the faithful, loving husband described in Hosea.

Matthew 5:7 tells us that "blessed are the merciful, for they will be shown mercy." As you become more immersed in Christlikeness you will begin to realize that you are practicing tenderness and mercy. Think of this calling as the elite branch and highest honor of serving God. We are God's ambassadors, bringing His message of healing to the world (2 Corinthians 5:20). Expert tenderness is needed when treating those who suffer with broken hearts and deep wounds, or when pursuing those who run the farthest from God. "Hosea work" is God's specialty. Psalm 147:2–3 assures us: "The Lord builds up Jerusalem; he gathers the exiles of Israel. He heals the brokenhearted and binds up their wounds."

God's comfort, compassion, and tender mercy are intended to be shared. *Compassion* means, "to suffer with." We receive this tenderness to pour it out to others who are in pain. This is the biblical chain of compassion: "Praise be to the God and Father of our Lord Jesus Christ, the Father of compassion and the God of all comfort, who comforts us in all our troubles, so that we can comfort those in any trouble with the comfort we ourselves receive from God" (2 Corinthians 1:3–4).

Note that our Father is the God of *all* comfort who can comfort us in *all* and *any* trouble. On the darkest day, God is sufficient to bind our deepest wounds. No problem or pain exists that is beyond God's reach. Paul and Timothy often needed

God's tenderness. When they arrived in Macedonia, they were exhausted, fearful, constantly harassed, embroiled in conflicts, and downcast.

> For when we came into Macedonia, we had no rest, but we were harassed at every turn—conflicts on the outside, fears within. But God, who comforts the downcast, comforted us by the coming of Titus, and not only by his coming but also by the comfort you had given him. He told us about your longing for me, your deep sorrow, your ardent concern for me, so that my joy was greater than ever.
>
> 2 Corinthians 7:5–7

God comforted them through *one person*, Titus. God sends individuals to pour tender compassion into the lives of discouraged and exhausted people. Compassionate tenderness is not a theology. It is an action. It comes in the form of real people sent by the God of all comfort.

Remember that God sent one real person to rescue and comfort us—Jesus, our merciful and faithful high priest (Hebrews 2:17). This was God's most tender act of compassion.

IS GOD ALWAYS GENTLE?

> He, Yahweh, is merciful, tenderhearted, slow to anger, very loving, and universally kind; Yahweh's tenderness embraces all his creatures.
>
> Psalm 145:8–9 TJB

We cannot leave this chapter without asking the difficult question, "But is God always gentle?" Is He always tender in the

Old Testament? Psalm 145:8–9 states that God is universally kind and that His tenderness embraces all His creatures. The New English Bible says: "The Lord is good to all men, and his tender care rests upon all his creatures." Anyone who has read the Old Testament with its continuous stream of violent deaths would probably disagree with the psalmist's view that God is tender with *all* his creatures. Is Scripture inaccurate on this subject?

Theologians have been wrestling with this seeming contradiction for centuries. God spoke the sixth commandment to Moses: "You shall not murder" (Exodus 20:13). Yet the Old Testament contains numerous accounts of killings and massacres, often as a result of God's doing or His direction. Many opponents of Christianity cite these examples as evidence of a violent, cruel God. Some say that God guided the Israelites to perform ethnic cleansing by eliminating their enemies. Events like these do not appear in the New Testament. We can understand why many Christians are comfortable holding in tension the wrath of the Old Testament God and the mercy of the New Testament God who came to us in the person of Jesus. "We are on the other side of Calvary," they offer, dismissing the perceived discrepancies. However, we cannot ignore this tension in a book about gentleness and our gentle Lord.

Romans 11:22 tells us to consider the kindness and sternness of God. We struggle to comprehend this dichotomy, but we must realize that God's thoughts are not our thoughts and God's ways are not our ways (Isaiah 55:8). We cannot compare God's ways and thoughts to ours. He loves us with an everlasting love and constant affection (Jeremiah 31:3). God proves throughout the Old Testament and in the New Testament story of Christ's crucifixion that He gives man every chance to have a relationship with him. He restrains himself to the last possible moment. Remember that gentleness is not weakness, but God will not tolerate evil indefinitely.

Scripture does not say that God is without anger. To relate to this in more recent history, imagine if countries had allowed Hitler to continue committing atrocities until he accomplished world domination. Would not stopping him have been an act of gentleness or would it have been sheer weakness and tolerance of rampant evil? I think we know that the gentler, kinder course of protecting innocent people was to make every effort to derail evil.

In my reading of Scripture, I find God to be more grief-stricken than angry with evil. Note His grief in Genesis 6 before flooding the earth: "When the Lord saw that man had done much evil on earth and that his thoughts and inclinations were always evil, he was sorry that he had made man on earth, and he was grieved at heart" (Genesis 6:5–6).

The classic Sunday school stories of Noah and Jonah are usually centered on the ark and the big fish. But there is so much more. In these passages lie key clues to our understanding of God's uniquely strong gentleness. God is passionate about having a relationship with even one man who seeks to follow Him. He saves Noah and his family because Noah is the "one blameless man of his time." Noah walks with God (Genesis 6:9 NEB).

Read Joshua 2 to see that God also saves Rahab, the prostitute, and her family from destruction because she trusted God and helped the Israelites. Scripture shows that God will move heaven and earth to protect a single person who wants a relationship with Him. He will restrain His power if there is any chance for repentance.

This fact made Jonah furious.

Jonah refuses to go to Nineveh when God asks Jonah to warn of coming destruction if the people of Nineveh do not repent of their evil ways. Jonah doesn't think they should be spared. They don't deserve it. He defiantly takes a detour through Joppa and the belly of a huge fish. Not given much of a choice, Jonah finally arrives in Nineveh and reluctantly preaches God's message. The people of Nineveh, including the king, repent and renounce their wickedness. "God saw their efforts to renounce their evil behavior. And God relented: he did not inflict on them the disaster which he had threatened" (Jonah 3:10 TJB).

In response Jonah has a raging tantrum. He is so angry with God that he no longer wants to live: "Yahweh, is not this just as I said would happen when I was still at home? That was why I went and fled to Tarshish: I knew that you were a God of tenderness and compassion, slow to anger, rich in graciousness, relenting from evil. So now Yahweh, please take away my life, for I might as well be dead as go on living" (Jonah 4:2–3 TJB).

God felt sorry for more than 120,000 lost people in Nineveh (Jonah 4:11) while Jonah wanted them destroyed. Jonah did not want to offer them any chance for repentance because he knew that his God is tender, compassionate, slow to anger, and gracious as He halts evil. God's character infuriates Jonah. At his lowest point, Jonah still stated truth we can count on.

Our God is tender and compassionate. He is gentle but not weak. He cannot tolerate evil indefinitely and allow it to flourish. God passionately pursues us. He will restrain His anger and power to give man every possible chance to follow Him. "He, Yahweh, is merciful, tenderhearted, slow to anger, very loving, and universally kind; Yahweh's tenderness embraces all his creatures" (Psalm 145:8–9 TJB).

Now you can reflect about whether Old Testament Scriptures about God's gentleness are inaccurate or misunderstood. You can also ponder whether you sometimes feel and act more like Jonah than Hosea. Then remember through all your life challenges how tender, kind, and loving God is with you.

> The main characteristic which is the proof of the indwelling Spirit is an amazing tenderness in personal dealing, and a blazing truthfulness with regard to God's Word.
>
> Oswald Chambers

Is there any encouragement from belonging to Christ? Any comfort from his love? Any fellowship together in the Spirit? Are your hearts tender and compassionate?

Philippians 2:1 NLT

PERSONAL RETREAT

• When has God been most tender with you?

• When have you felt pursued by God during a bleak spiritual season?

- When has God called you to extend love and tenderness to an unusually difficult person? Have you ever practiced "Hosea love" in someone's life?

- Is your heart tender and compassionate (Philippians 2:1)? When have you been the human face of God's tender comfort and compassion for a harassed friend? Have you been someone's Titus?

- Read Isaiah 54:7–10 to reflect on God's everlasting love and His restraint of anger. How do you wrestle with God's character as described by Jonah contrasted with violent Old Testament events?

Nothing is so strong as gentleness, nothing so gentle as real strength.

—Saint Francis de Sales

Jesus was called a friend of sinners, relentlessly pursuing the downtrodden. What an irony that today his followers are seen in the opposite light!

—David Kinnaman

Any Christ-shaped calling is cross-shaped.

—Andy Crouch

3

IS JESUS MEEK AND MILD?

Gentle Jesus, meek and mild, Look upon a little child; Pity my simplicity, Suffer me to come to Thee.

—*Charles Wesley*

*I*magine a gentle, kind, humble, peaceful, and soft-spoken person. Now, could you also picture this same person as strong, fearless, a person of action, a dynamic leader, a powerful speaker, a protector of the weak, and a mover and shaker who changes history?

The two images collide. We can't imagine these qualities coalesced . . . until we meet Jesus.

If we are honest, we don't like the image of a meek Messiah who appears weak any more than the Pharisees of Jesus' day did. They wanted the Messiah to be a powerful leader who ushered in a new age on earth. However, Jesus came from humble beginnings and was not a political or military leader. Jesus did not come to change the political world of the first century but to transform individual lives for eternity. To the Pharisees, Jesus was first a disappointment, then a joke, and finally a threat.

You may bristle like I do at the "meek and mild" image of Jesus that Charles Wesley described in his well-known hymn, "Gentle Jesus, Meek and Mild." The Christmas Eve presentation of helpless baby Jesus in the manger, when separated from the death-defying resurrected Lord we celebrate on Easter, can rankle us. I want to tell people that our powerful Lord did not remain a "meek and mild" infant.

JESUS' ANGER

Scripture reveals that our "meek and mild" Savior became angry. He became furious when He came upon money changers in the temple area who profited from selling animals for sacrifice and who took advantage of the poor. Jesus overturned their tables and benches, accused them of being robbers, and drove them with a whip of cords from the temple (John 2:15). This scene has prompted some to ask, "Could Jesus be violent?" Is this our gentle Lord?

> Jesus entered the temple area and drove out all who were buying and selling there. He overturned the tables of the money-changers and the benches of those selling doves. "It is written," he said to them, " 'My house will be called a house of prayer,' but you are making it a 'den of robbers.' "
>
> Matthew 21:12

Neither is Jesus gentle, meek, or mild when He exerts His power over Satan and speaks sternly to the enemy of our souls.

> In the synagogue there was a man possessed by a demon, an impure spirit. He cried out at the top of his voice, "Go away! What do you want with us, Jesus of Nazareth? Have you come to destroy us? I know who you are—the Holy One of God!" "Be quiet!" Jesus said sternly. "Come out of him!" Then the demon threw the man down before them all and came out without injuring him.
>
> Luke 4:33–35

He then began to teach them that the Son of Man must suffer many things and be rejected by the elders, the chief priests and the teachers of the law, and that he must be killed and after three days rise again. He spoke plainly about this, and Peter took him aside and began to rebuke him. But when Jesus turned and looked at his disciples, he rebuked Peter. "Get behind me, Satan!" he said. "You do not have in mind the concerns of God, but merely human concerns."

Mark 8:31–33

We observe that Jesus bucks the hypocritical establishment and speaks harshly and honestly to the teachers of the law and Pharisees throughout the gospels. In Matthew 23:23–36, he calls them vicious names: "You blind guides! . . . You snakes! You brood of vipers! . . . You are like whitewashed tombs, which look beautiful on the outside but on the inside are full of dead men's bones and everything unclean." If someone verbally attacked you like this, I'm sure you would describe it: "He yelled at me and called me horrible names." Is this gentle Jesus?

When the Pharisees confront Jesus for healing a man's shriveled hand on the Sabbath, Jesus is angry with them and deeply distressed by their stubbornness (Mark 3:1–6). This heated exchange is serious enough to prompt the Pharisees to begin plotting his death.

Lest we identify with Jesus when we lose our tempers, we need to realize that Jesus' behavior while displaying righteous anger was the exception, not the rule. He was unusually patient and gentle with His disciples and followers. Jesus became angry only in two types of situations:

- with Satan or satanic spirits.
- with people who claimed to follow God but were hypocrites, especially teachers of the law who imposed obstacles to people's faith in God.

If you only remember one sentence from this book, may this be it: **Jesus was never angry or harsh with lost, broken people.**

JESUS' COMPASSION

Jesus poured out infinite compassion, gentleness, love, and kindness into the lives of hurting people. Jesus patiently listened to them. He spent time with them. He taught them. He fed them. He healed them. He protected them. He grieved with them. Jesus was *filled with compassion* for suffering people (Mark 1:41).

> Jesus went through all the towns and villages, teaching in their synagogues, preaching the good news of the kingdom and healing every disease and sickness. When he saw the crowds, he had compassion on them, because they were harassed and helpless, like sheep without a shepherd.
> Matthew 9:35–36

This is my favorite example of Jesus' compassion for hurting people:

> As he approached the town gate, a dead person was being carried out—the only son of his mother, and she was a widow. And a large crowd from the town was with her. When the Lord saw her, his heart went out to her and he

said, "Don't cry." Then he went up and touched the bier they were carrying him on, and the bearers stood still. He said, "Young man, I say to you, get up!" The dead man sat up and began to talk, and Jesus gave him back to his mother.

Luke 7:12–15

We can only imagine the depths of this widow's pain as she grieved for her only son. Jesus' heart went out to her, and he said, "Don't cry." He felt her pain, then He healed her son. The NKJV translates "his heart went out to her" as "he had compassion on her." Jesus' compassion was so deep that he was moved to eliminate her pain. Philip Yancey sums up our Lord's compassionate heart: "Jesus gives God a face, and that face is streaked with tears." [1]

We Have a Gentle, Restrained Lord

Come to me, all you who are weary and burdened, and I will give you rest. Take my yoke upon you and learn from me, for I am gentle and humble in heart, and you will find rest for your souls. For my yoke is easy and my burden is light.

Matthew 11:28–30

Jesus describes His lordship as gentle. His heart is humble. Paul appeals to the Corinthians "by the meekness and gentleness of Christ" (2 Corinthians 10:1). Perhaps Jesus Christ was meek and mild in the true sense of those words.

When Jesus Christ quietly accepted execution without defending himself, restraining himself from destroying the tormentors who repeatedly tried to provoke Him, He unleashed God's divine grace to rescue you and me from the clutches of death. He restrained himself out of love for us. Observe when Jesus restrained his power instead of unleashing His fury:

Jesus restrained His power when he was arrested.
Do you think I cannot call on my Father, and he will at once put at my disposal more than twelve legions of angels? But how then would the Scriptures be fulfilled that say it must happen in this way?

Matthew 26:53–54

Jesus restrained His power before the Sanhedrin.
"He is worthy of death," they answered. Then they spit in his face and struck him with their fists. Others slapped him and said, "Prophesy to us, Messiah. Who hit you?"

Matthew 26:66–68

Jesus restrained His power with the soldiers.
The men who were guarding Jesus began mocking and beating him. They blindfolded him and demanded, "Prophesy! Who hit you?" And they said many other insulting things to him.

Luke 22:63–65

The soldiers also came up and mocked him. They offered him wine vinegar and said, "If you are the king of the Jews, save yourself."

Luke 23:36–37

Then Jesus restrained His power as He died on a cross like a criminal. We can reflect Him only if we understand this countercultural and counterintuitive biblical Jesus.

If a "gentle, meek, and mild" person still sounds like a weak, passive doormat to you, then remember that Jesus Christ restrained His strength and exerted power under control for a greater, eternal purpose. The salvation of the world depended on His gentle restraint. But His restraint was not the end of the story. It forged the path for Him to immerse broken people in His grace and love.

Gently Loving the Unlovable

Jesus went out and saw a tax collector by the name of Levi sitting at his tax booth. "Follow me," Jesus said to him, and Levi got up, left everything and followed him. Then Levi held a great banquet for Jesus at his house, and a large crowd of tax collectors and others were eating with them. But the Pharisees and the teachers of the law who belonged to their sect complained to his disciples, "Why do you eat and drink with tax collectors and sinners?" Jesus answered them, "It is not the healthy who need a doctor, but the sick. I have not come to call the righteous, but sinners to repentance."

Luke 5:27–32

The Pharisees were appalled that Jesus spent time with tax collectors and prostitutes. Tax collectors and money-lenders in biblical times were considered the scum of society. They became rich by charging their fellow Jews extra fees and interest. Think of them as loan sharks.

The Pharisees knew that Jesus was not preaching to these lost people or holding classes for them. He was hanging out with them. He was eating meals in their homes. He was treating them like friends. Jesus' behavior disgusted the Pharisees. They described Jesus as a "glutton and a drunkard, a friend of tax collectors and sinners" (Luke 7:34).

If Jesus walked our streets today, perhaps he would be hanging out with addicts, drug lords, pimps, prostitutes, organized crime bosses, or Wall Street crooks. He would be meeting in bars with people who were looking for one-night stands. He would not necessarily be inviting them to outreaches or seminars in churches. He would be going into their homes in some of the most dangerous parts of our cities. He would be extending genuine friendship as He spent time getting to know them and they got to know Him—all the while He would offer them the gift of His unconditional love and healing.

We might view Jesus' behavior as "coming down to their level," but then we miss the point. There was not a single hint of Jesus' superiority or arrogance. The all-knowing and all-powerful God was not patronizing or condescending. Jesus was the essence of gentle humility. He did not simply "tolerate" these people or just "minister to them." He loved them and they felt it—despite the Pharisees' disapproval.

The Pharisees were equally appalled when a "sinful woman" poured perfume on Jesus' feet as He reclined at the table: "she came there with an alabaster jar of perfume. As she stood behind him at his feet weeping, she began to wet his feet with her tears. Then she wiped them with her hair, kissed them and poured perfume on them" (Luke 7:37–38).

Simon, the Pharisee who was Jesus' host, said, "If this man were a prophet, he would know who is touching him and what kind of woman she is—that she is a sinner" (Luke 7:39). We might surmise that this woman was known for her sexual sins. She didn't just pour perfume on Jesus' feet as he lay back and relaxed. She poured it in very sensual ways, wiping his feet with her hair and kissing him as other men watched. And Jesus did not stop her or reprimand her.

Instead he reprimanded Simon: "Do you see this woman? I came into your house. You did not give me any water for my feet, but she wet my feet with her tears and wiped them with her hair. You did not give me a kiss, but this woman, from the time I entered, has not stopped kissing my feet. You did not put oil on my head, but she has poured perfume on my feet. Therefore, I tell you, her many sins have been forgiven—as her great love has shown. But whoever has been forgiven little loves little" (Luke 7:44–47).

This sensual woman did not stop kissing Jesus' feet from the time he entered Simon's house. Imagine how arousing that act appeared. Jesus graciously appreciated her gift and tenderly forgave her.

The Pharisees assumed the worst about Jesus. To bring this closer to home, imagine that you see your pastor enter a bar known to be frequented by drug addicts and prostitutes. Would you assume the worst about your pastor?

Do we resemble Jesus or the Pharisees?

Gentleness is power under perfect control.
—Stanley Horton

Lamb of God, I look to Thee; Thou shalt my
Example be; Thou art gentle, meek, and mild;
Thou wast once a little child. . . . Loving Jesus,
gentle Lamb, In Thy gracious hands I am;
Make me, Savior, what Thou art, Live Thyself
within my heart.

—Charles Wesley

PERSONAL RETREAT

• How often do you observe our culture equating following Jesus' example of being "gentle, meek, and mild" with
being a passive, spineless doormat?

• Reflect on the instances when Jesus unleashed His temper
(overturning tables in the temple area and driving the sell-
ers out with a whip or verbally attacking the Pharisees).
Now contrast that wrath with the gentle restraint and
control Jesus showed when His tormentors abused Him
as He faced a torturous death. He could have destroyed
them. When have you received or poured out gentleness
presented as harnessed strength?

- How can we be as gentle and gracious as our Lord and find opportunities to pour His compassion into the lives around us, especially with hurting people?

- Think of a place where Jesus would spend time with unlovable people today that would offend you. Who is going in His place?

We were created for kind and gentle living. . . . When Christians fail to measure up to the standards of kindness and gentleness, we are not the people God meant us to be.

—Richard Mouw

I want Christians to be known as the most loving people—the kind of people who love you until it hurts. But so far it seems like we're bringing more hurt than healing to many.

—Margaret Feinberg

It is no great matter to associate with the good and gentle, for this is naturally pleasing to all, and everyone willingly enjoys peace and loves best those who agree with them. But to live peacefully with people who are hard, perverse, disorderly, or contrary to us is a great grace and a most commendable courageous thing.

—Thomas à Kempis

4

ARE CHRISTIANS KNOWN
FOR BEING GENTLE?

But you, man of God, flee from all this, and pursue righteousness,
godliness, faith, love, endurance and gentleness. Fight the good fight
of the faith.

1 Timothy 6:11–12

*N*ow that we have observed what biblical gentleness looks like,
we are ready to ask the tough question, "Are Christians known
for being gentle in our world?" We also need to ask the more
personal question, "Am *I* known for being gentle?"

Paul encourages us in 1 Timothy 6:11 to pursue righteousness, godliness, faith, love, endurance, and gentleness in order
to "Fight the good fight of faith" (v. 12). John summarizes
this calling in his letters as living a "life of love." The imagery may seem incongruent. Yet we are called to engage in a
gentle fight in which our most powerful weapons are gentleness and tender love in action. When we see angry Christians
fighting in defense of their faith and values, we note that Paul
did not write, "Fight *for* our faith." We also do not fight for
our salvation. That fight has already been fought and won by
Jesus Christ. In his insightful book *Uncommon Decency: Chris-*
tian Civility in an Uncivil World Richard Mouw writes, "The

world has already been visited by one overwhelmingly adequate Messiah. No more would-be messiahs need apply."[1]

A Troubling Reputation

The sad reality is that the healing touch of Christ's gentleness and kindness seems to be sorely lacking today. It's become ironic that the term *evangelical* has its roots in "bringing good news," because these "bad news" reputations are too often associated with Christians:

- Opinionated
- Arrogant
- Argumentative
- Judgmental
- Angry
- Harsh
- Rude
- Obnoxious
- Hyperpolitical
- Intolerant
- Bigoted
- Homophobic
- Hypocritical
- Narrow-minded

I have gleaned these common descriptors of Christians from inside and outside the church community. I know Christians who do not reveal their faith to acquaintances or new friends until their relationships are established. They do this to prevent being written off as angry, intolerant fanatics. I thought, or at least hoped, that my findings about Christians were unusual—until I read the book *Unchristian* by David Kinnaman, president of the Barna Group. He says that Christianity has an image problem and that our faith is at a turning point in America.[2] In his research with non-Christian young people, ages 16–29, he found that 38 percent claim to have a bad impression of Christianity and 49 percent have a worse impression of evangelical Christianity. One-third of this group thinks Christianity has a negative image with which they do not want to be associated.[3]

I mistakenly assumed that these negative impressions of Christians were most influenced by stereotypes in film and television or news media reports showing angry Christians picketing abortion clinics or marching in anti-gay rallies. I was saddened to learn in *Unchristian* that most young people form their negative impressions of Christianity through interacting and conversing with individual Christians. One-fifth of this group had a painful experience in a church that turned them off to Jesus Christ. Kinnaman observes that young people reject Christ because they feel rejected by Christians.[4]

An article entitled "Are Christians More Like Jesus or More Like the Pharisees?" details a new Barna Group study that measured qualities most resembling Christ in a nationwide sample of self-identified Christians. This study reveals the following: 51 percent of Christians practice the attitudes and actions of pharisaical behavior while 14 percent practice the attitudes and actions of Jesus Christ. Thirty-five percent of the Christians sampled practice a mixture of Christlike behavior and pharisaical attitude.

Kinnaman explains, "This research may help to explain how evangelicals are often targeted for claims of hypocrisy; the unique 'sin' of evangelicals tends to be doing the right things but with improper motives." Research conducted for *unchristian* showed that 84 percent of young non-Christians said that they knew a Christian personally, while only 15 percent said that they knew a Christian whose behavior was different in a positive way.[5]

All these statistics remind me of my own journey exploring the Christian faith as a young person before I became a follower of Jesus Christ in college. Throughout high school, I was taken to countless Bible studies and church services (complete with altar calls) by friends who attended church. I found their heated arguments with me about religion tiresome. When their unchristian behavior during the week didn't line up with the faith they were espousing, I was confused. When people say, "Christians are the biggest deterrent to people knowing God," I understand their experience.

PERCEPTION VERSUS REALITY

If Christ were here now there is one thing he would not be—a Christian.

—Mark Twain

I could understand negative perceptions of Christians based on media stereotypes. Knowing that the perceptions are based in reality is hard to accept. For instance, young people working on staff at a well-known Christian conference center shared with me one summer that sometimes the most respected, popular speakers who drew the largest crowds were also the most impatient and rude to staff members. Others working in the service industry on a cruise ship have told me that often Christian groups are the most demanding customers and the stingiest tippers. Some servers have described Christians who dine at their restaurants after Sunday church services as their most ungracious patrons. One young female server who is a Christian said, "Could they please just not talk about church if they are going to be rude? It's a terrible witness to the restaurant staff."

Within the church, when a woman named Candace finally braved telling her close friend that her son revealed he is gay, her friend's immediate response was, "What are you going to do about that? You know he's going to hell."

When Lisa's son developed a drug problem and her teen-age daughter became pregnant, Lisa knew that church members were gossiping about her poor parenting skills under the guise of praying for her. One father went to the church board, asking that Lisa's children be excluded from the church youth group because they were a dangerous influence.

When Marie's husband left her for another woman, she was immediately dismissed from her church leadership position and discouraged from attending functions for couples.

Several friends have told me that when they were experiencing a tough time in life, such as a divorce, family member's addiction, or teen pregnancy, non-Christian friends were kinder and gentler than Christians who attended their church. They received more grace, understanding, and compassion from non-Christians than Christians. Outside the church was a safer place to heal than inside the church. One pastor who noticed this disease of "ungrace" in his church told me, "Every human being hungers to be fully known and unconditionally loved. This is what God does for us. My challenge is helping my church members to do the same for each other. The church seems to be the toughest place to be vulnerable."

How is it that Christians called to dispense the aroma of grace instead emit the noxious fumes of ungrace?

—Philip Yancey

OUR BIBLICAL CALLING

Now compare the list of negative Christian reputations and behaviors with our biblical calling to bear fruit: "But the fruit of the Spirit is love, joy, peace, forebearance, kindness, goodness, faithfulness, gentleness and self-control" (Galatians 5:22–23).

Being gentle or tender requires also being patient, kind, restrained, and self-controlled. These qualities are the visible behaviors that allow us to pour God's grace, love, joy, peace, goodness, and faithfulness into the world. Practicing these qualities are the tangible ways that we show Christ's love. Paul tells us in 1 Corinthians 13:4–5 that love is

- Patient
- Kind
- Humble (not boastful, proud, or envious)
- Courteous (not rude)
- Generous (not selfish)
- Calm and peaceful (not angry)

What do you notice when you compare the lists? Does the initial list look like weaknesses gone wild? Now imagine how daily practicing the Christlike gentle traits would have an impact on our world as well as transform the intimate relationships within our own families.

Can one be a Christian and be an impatient, rude person? Yes. Can one be a Christian and be a thoughtless, harsh person? Yes. Can one be a Christian and be an arrogant, argumentative person? Yes. Can one be a Christian and have a bad temper? Yes.

Can one be a Christian and experience road rage? Yes. Driving behaviors simply reveal our gut reactions when people stand in the way of what we want. Gary laughed as he told me that he doesn't put Christian bumper stickers on his car because he doesn't want other drivers to know that he is a Christian when he loses his temper. "That would be a bad witness," he explained. Gary apparently doesn't see that changing his behavior would be the better solution.

Then Gary added, "We all fall short of the glory of God. We are all broken, sinful people and that's why we need a Savior." He stated a biblical fact that is the crux of our faith.

Can one be an unkind person devoid of gentleness and still be saved? Yes.

But the fruit is rotten. And the world is watching.

So where are the gentle Christians today? Do they exist?

When Gentleness Melts Barriers

Christians are primarily perceived for what they stand against. We have become famous for what we oppose, rather than who we are for.

—David Kinnaman

Gentle Christians are known for who they represent, instead of what they stand against. Leaving aside statistics and reputations, I can tell you that I know many Christlike people who daily practice His gentleness and share His love with the world. You are probably thinking of the ones you know. Due to their quiet spirit, they fly under the radar, not calling attention to themselves. Yet they change people's misperceptions of Christians. Their gentleness melts barriers and builds bridges as they take to heart Scripture's command to be gentle with *all* people (Titus 3:2) and kind to *everyone* (2 Timothy 2:24).

Rob, a pastor, explains his approach of treating every person who crosses his path with gentleness as, "I am a coach but not the umpire." He shared with me that a few years ago a gay couple moved into the house next door to the home he shares with his wife. When the couple learned that Rob was a pastor, they immediately started building a seven-feet-high fence between their properties. They assumed that a Christian pastor would be hostile toward them. Rob was determined to befriend his neighbors, so he offered to help build the fence and pay for half the cost. In the process of building the fence together, they became close friends. Rob started helping them with all their house repair projects. Rob attended their parties and invited the couple to dine at his home. He became acquainted with their gay friends and community. When they press him about spiritual matters, he gently explains his beliefs. When they asked him to conduct a ceremony to bless their legal union, he declined but offered to help host the reception. Rob knows that some of his church board members would disapprove of his friendship with his neighbors. But he also knows that Christ would have befriended them.

When Gentleness Melts Opposition

Our job is to love others without stopping to inquire whether or not they are worthy.

—Thomas Merton

For years I had heard people praise the gentle homicide detective, Dan Wolke, who lived out his faith in the toughest circumstances with the most unlovable people. After an impressive career as inspector with the Berkeley Police Department, he retired and became a chaplain with the police department in his hometown. When I interviewed Dan, I pressed him to tell me the practical ways he mirrored Christ's love and how he treated hardcore criminals with gentleness, kindness, and respect. He said it wasn't easy, especially when he was investigating kidnappings or other crimes against children. His life experiences could be a manual for the scriptural journey we are sharing in this book.

Wolke learned early in his career that bullying people with brute force did not help anyone. He tried to be as gentle and considerate with the perpetrators of crimes as he was with the victims and their families. He provided a godly example and ministered to fellow police officers. After arresting criminals, he treated them as he would want to be treated—with dignity and respect. He spoke to criminals without judging them. He listened to them and gave them the gift of silence when needed. He offered to pray with criminals and explained, "I have struggles. I am a sinner too." He offered them the lifeline of God's hope and forgiveness with no strings attached. Wolke tried to share God's tenderness by communicating, "God never gives up on us." He spoke the same message into the pain and brokenness of victims' lives and added, "I will stay with you until you ask me to leave. You are not alone."

In one unique case, Wolke reached out to a heroin addict who had committed numerous armed robberies and had made repeated trips to prison. He learned while talking to the young man's parents that his father was a chief of police in another state. Throughout the years, Wolke corresponded with this young man, visited him in prison, and sent him a Bible and Christian books. Dan prayed with him as well as for him, leading him to trust in Jesus Christ before he died in a prison hospital.

Wolke told me, "One key to practicing gentleness is humility. In my work, I need to get out of the way so that hurting people can see more of Christ and less of me. Another key is embracing the opportunity God offers us to give Him our entire hearts."

Dan Wolke's words remind me of Paul's plea to the Corinthians to "open wide your hearts" (2 Corinthians 6:13). Wolke's example encourages us because he daily practiced a life of gentleness with everyone, regardless of their circumstances.

Southern California pastor Dave Gibbons said, "Christian love ought to involve being a gentle conversationalist with the world."[6] Pastor Rob and Dan Wolke are living examples of Christ's followers who conduct gentle conversations with people in the world who perceive them as enemies and who are then surprised to be on the receiving end of God's love and tenderness. Antonio Anderson calls this "Christian surprise-love."

Gentleness with Enemies

Antonio Anderson pastors a church in Mexico near the border, helping poor people in the barrios and loving their enemy, the shockingly violent cartel. Some of the young men who have disappeared into organized crime are children of his church families. Anderson and his congregation previously prayed only for the kidnapped and murdered innocents, but after studying Jesus' example in Scripture, they now also pray for the assassins and reach out to them:

> The world holds these criminals in utter disdain. They are human garbage and social scabs. When they hear that there are some of us who love them, who are praying and fasting for them, their jaws drop. This Christian surprise-love has led to miraculous conversions among them.[7]

Jesus tells us, "Love your enemies, do good to those who hate you, bless those who curse you, pray for those who mistreat you" (Luke 6:27–28). Why would Jesus need to admonish us to be kind to people who are kind to us? It is our natural human response to return to others what we receive from them, which can as easily lead to revenge as kindness. Note that Jesus did not instruct us: "Tolerate your enemies" or "Don't harm your enemies, simply avoid them." He wants us to love our enemies, extending ourselves to embrace them. We are called to be gracious to everyone around us, pouring God's infinite grace into their lives with gentle kindness, courtesy, and compassion. Stanley Horton says that the best translation of "gentleness" in our English language is "kindness." Then he writes that the best translation of "kindness" is returning good for evil.[8] The truest test of gentleness is sharing it with people who treat us as enemies.

An enemy can be someone who opposes you. Whom do you consider your enemy? Someone who disagrees with you . . . an acquaintance who avoids you . . . the neighbor who won't speak to you . . . the store clerk who was rude to you . . . the trusted friend who gossiped about you . . . the spouse who betrayed you . . . the coworker who slandered you . . . the criminal who assaulted you . . . the terrorist on the other side of the world who plots to maim and kill innocent people? Who is hostile to you? A furious elderly parent suffering with dementia or an angry teenage child?

Whether we are reacting to the slightest offense or the deepest wound, we are called to envelope everyone, including our enemies, with prayer, compassion, love, kindness, respect, and gentleness. When enemies do not directly cross our path, we can still cover them with daily prayer. Jesus said, "Pray for those who mistreat you" (Luke 6:28). When offering the love of Christ to enemies that do cross our path, Jesus calls us to actively "do good to those who hate you, bless those who curse you" (6:27–28). "Turning one's cheek" (Luke 6:29) is the ultimate act of strength, restraint, kindness, and courageous gentleness.

Where are you on the gentleness continuum? Are you more known for "bad news" behaviors, or are you known for melting barriers like Rob, Dan, and Antonio have done? Most of us are in the middle of the continuum. If you find our calling to practice gentleness with all people to be challenging, you will be comforted to know that God can soften anyone into a gentle person. In the next chapter, we will see how He transformed this harsh, bitter, extremely ungentle man named Paul.

There is no sinner without a future, just as there is no saint without a past.

—Antonio Anderson

PERSONAL RETREAT

- In your own experience and circle of contacts, what do you observe is the reputation of Christians? Do you agree that they are known more for what they oppose than who they stand for? What are you known for?

- Think about your own journey of faith or the spiritual journey of someone you care about. Did Christians point away from God or toward God? Did they mirror Christ or the Pharisees? You probably had different experiences with different Christians.

- In the coming weeks, how can you become a gentle conversationalist with the world? How can you shower people with Christian surprise-love?

- Think about people who perceive you as an enemy or you perceive them as an enemy. Can you graciously extend the gentle love of Christ to embrace them? Reflect on Proverbs 16:7 (TJB): "Let Yahweh be pleased with a man's way of life and he makes his very enemies into friends."

- Read Luke 6:32–33: "If you love those who love you, what credit is that to you? Even sinners love those who love them. And if you do good to those who are good to you, what credit is that to you? Even sinners do that." We are called to the tough work of returning good for evil, to love people who would do us harm. Think about how gentleness and kindness are the anchors of our calling.

- Think about an enemy who does not cross your path. Can you daily pray for him or her?

Endeavor to be patient in enduring the failures and weaknesses of others, no matter what kind they are, for you yourself have many failings that must be endured by others.

—Thomas à Kempis

Treating other people with the gentleness and reverence of Jesus requires that we be deeply sensitive to the pain and brokenness of a creation that has not yet been fully delivered from its cursedness.

—Richard Mouw

5

WHAT HAPPENED TO SAUL?

While they were stoning him, Stephen prayed, "Lord, Jesus, receive my spirit." Then he fell on his knees and cried out, "Lord, do not hold this sin against them." When he had said this, he fell asleep. And Saul approved of their killing him. . . . Godly men buried Stephen and mourned deeply for him. But Saul began to destroy the church. Going from house to house, he dragged off men and women and put them in prison.

Acts 7:59–8:1–3

*W*ould you consider Paul an example of gentleness? I doubt it. You may be surprised to learn that Paul's letters include more instructions to be gentle than any other part of Scripture. I believe this is because Paul was not naturally gentle. When Saul was murdering Christians before he was transformed into Paul, he was angry, arrogant, harsh, and cruel. Saul was a monster.

After Stephen testified before the Sanhedrin, the listeners were furious! They ground and grind their teeth at him, becoming a violent, screaming mob. Saul incited them to rush at Stephen, drag him out of the city, strip him, and stone him to death (Acts 7:54–8:1). Saul set in motion a horrendous persecution as he went from house to house, dragged men and women off to prison and terrorized families. Christians were terrified of him.

Acts 9:1–2 tells us that Saul continued to breathe out murderous threats against the Lord's disciples. He asked for letters to the synagogues from the high priest so he could take any Christian men or women to Jerusalem to imprison them.

When the Lord tells Ananias to find Saul and "place his hands on him to restore his sight" (v. 12), Ananias answers: "Lord, . . . I have heard many reports about this man and all the harm he has done to your holy people in Jerusalem. And he has come here with authority from the chief priests to arrest all who call on your name" (Acts 9:13–14).

It is no wonder that the early Christians doubted Paul's conversion. It probably sounded like a trick designed to trap them. Imagine if you learned that a violent dictator or sadistic serial killer had been pardoned and asked to accept a leadership position in your church. Would you trust him?

The people who heard Paul preach after he spent time with the disciples were astonished. They asked, "Isn't he the man who raised havoc in Jerusalem and among those who call on this name? And hasn't he come here to take them as prisoners to the chief priests?" (Acts 9:21). The bolder Paul became in preaching Jesus Christ, the more baffled the people were. When Paul tried to join the disciples in Jerusalem, they "were all afraid of him, not believing that he really was a disciple" (Acts 9:26).

Even after coming face-to-face with the living Christ, Paul was not noted for being gentle. Is this the same person who wrote in Colossians to be clothed in compassion, kindness, humility, gentleness, and patience? This transformation was hard work for Paul. Through his letters, we observe a man who is slowly maturing in Christ. Paul is our best example of a man struggling to reflect his Lord. We can relate to his journey. It was a process for him just as it is for us. We may be saved in a moment, but we do not become Christlike in a moment. If God can transform Paul into Christ's image, He can change anyone.

The monster who cruelly murdered Christians became so gentle that he was like a mother caring for her little children. He overflowed with love to reflect his tenderhearted Father. Can this be the man who killed Stephen?

> As apostles of Christ we could have asserted our authority. Instead, we were like young children among you. Just as a nursing mother cares for her children, so we cared for you. Because we loved you so much, we were delighted to share with you not only the gospel of God but our lives as well.
>
> 1 Thessalonians 2:7–8

PAUL'S STRUGGLES

Paul was being transformed, but he was not perfect. Even as a converted follower of Jesus Christ, he was usually embroiled in conflicts with the authorities or other Christians. I would imagine that when either of those groups saw Paul approaching, they thought, "Here comes trouble." He wreaked havoc in a new way.

I believe that God honors the natural bent of a person He has fashioned. Each of us is one of God's unique creations. When God rescues us, He does not alter our core temperament. He transforms it into a whole, healthy reflection of Him and uses it for His glorious purposes. Converted Paul remained the same strong, determined man with a new life mission—to preach the gospel and love Christians instead of destroying them.

Yet he was still a bulldozer. It's no wonder that Paul keeps reminding his readers to be gentle, because he needs to constantly remember this too. He seems to assume that other

Christians struggle with being gentle and kind as much as he does. Even Paul's letters hurt and frighten his readers (2 Corinthians 7:8, 10:9), and he doesn't regret his harsh approach.

Paul's second consistent reminder throughout his letters is to lead quiet, peaceful lives. Being quiet and peaceful is also a struggle for Paul. As you read the following relational advice regarding gentleness, remember that being gentle and peaceful is not Paul's natural bent. Note that being gentle is often linked to not being quarrelsome. Paul certainly knew how to stir up conflict and argue, and he realized that one cannot be both a gentle person and an argumentative person.

Paul's Advice

Remember Paul's history as you read his guidance. I'm sure these lessons were gleaned in painful ways as the troublemaker Paul learned what *not* to do in different situations. Often the best person to help us with a specific problem is someone who experienced it before overcoming it. For example, if you know a recovering alcoholic who attends Alcoholics Anonymous, you also know that he or she has a sponsor who is a recovering alcoholic. If you struggle with gentleness, think of Paul as your sponsor.

Be gentle to all. Paul calls us to be gentle toward all people, including the government and authorities.

Remind them to be submissive to the government and the authorities, to obey them, and to be ready for any honourable form of work; to slander no one, *not to pick quarrels,* to show forbearance and a *consistently gentle disposition towards all men.*

Titus 3:1–2 NEB

Be kind to everyone. Just as Paul instructs us to be gentle toward all men, he tells us to be kind to *everyone*. We do not get to pick which people we should treat well. Our gracious behavior is to be consistent with everyone, from our family and fellow Christians to strangers or adversaries in our world. We are called to gently instruct those who oppose us, realizing that only God changes hearts.

> Don't have anything to do with foolish and stupid arguments, because you know they produce quarrels. And the Lord's servant *must not be quarrelsome* but must be *kind to everyone*, able to teach, not resentful. *Opponents must be gently instructed*, in the hope that God will grant them repentance leading them to a knowledge of the truth, and that they will come to their senses and escape from the trap of the devil, who has taken them captive to do his will.
>
> 2 Timothy 2:23–25

Be gentle leaders. Paul calls leaders to be gentle and self-controlled. They are expected to be respectable because they have earned that respect.

> Now the overseer is to be above reproach, faithful to his wife, temperate, self-controlled, respectable, hospitable, able to teach, not given to drunkenness, *not violent but gentle, not quarrelsome*, not a lover of money.
>
> 1 Timothy 3:2–3

Gently guide strugglers. Paul asks us to carry each other's burdens and gently guide struggling Christians who are trapped in sin. Lest we be judgmental or arrogant, we must realize that we can be tempted too.

> Brothers and sisters, if someone is caught in a sin, *you who live by the Spirit should restore that person gently.* But watch yourselves, or you also may be tempted. Carry each other's burdens, and in this way you will fulfill the law of Christ.
>
> Galatians 6:1

Be completely humble. In Ephesians 4:2, Paul does not write "be a little humble and gentle" or "sometimes be humble and gentle." Paul writes, "Be completely humble and gentle."

> As a prisoner for the Lord, then, I urge you to live a life worthy of the calling you have received. *Be completely humble and gentle*; be patient, bearing with one another in love. Make every effort to keep the unity of the Spirit through the bond of peace
>
> Ephesians 4:1–3

This is what the love of Christ looks like. Whether we are working with government officials or other authorities, relating to people who oppose us and our beliefs, trying to help believers who have lost their way, or are leading others, we are called to practice gentleness and kindness. When? In all situations. How? By being completely gentle. With whom? Everyone.

There is no confusion about our calling. It is easy to understand, yet incredibly difficult to practice. Paul knew that better than anyone.

Follow my example, as I follow the example of Christ. I praise you for remembering me in everything and for holding to the traditions just as I passed them on to you.

1 Corinthians 11:1–2

PERSONAL RETREAT

- Can you identify with Paul's struggles to tame his anger and quarrelsome streak to imitate Christ and be gentle with all people and kind to everyone?

- Compare Paul's description of *love* in 1 Corinthians 13:4–5 with the *New American Oxford Dictionary*'s definition of *gentle*: "kind, courteous, chivalrous, not harsh or severe." A gentleman (or gentlewoman) is a kind, tender, gracious, thoughtful, and courteous person. Reflect on how Jesus was the ultimate "gentleman," and we are called to imitate His example.

- When is it most difficult for you to practice gentleness? Think of the most challenging people in your circle of "everyone" and ponder how to apply Paul's advice to someone:
  - who has authority over you.
  - who opposes you (and your faith) and provokes arguments.
  - that you lead and have authority over him/her.
  - who is struggling with his/her faith and obedience to Christ.
  - who tests you to be completely humble, gentle, and patient.

Father, I beg you to keep me in this silence so that I may learn from it the word of your peace and the word of your mercy and the word of your gentleness to the world: and that through me perhaps your word of peace may make itself heard where it has not been possible for anyone to hear it for a long time.

—Thomas Merton

God wants nothing of you but the gift of a peaceful heart.

—Meister Eckhart

We are not at peace with others because we are not at peace with ourselves, and we are not at peace with ourselves because we are not at peace with God.

—Thomas Merton

6

PRACTICING A GENTLE AND QUIET SPIRIT

Blessed are the ears that eagerly listen for the breath of the divine whisper, and do not pay attention to the many whisperings of the world.

Thomas à Kempis

*T*his beautiful sentiment from Thomas à Kempis' book *The Imitation of Christ* sums up the essence of a gentle and quiet spirit. God longs for us to be so sensitive to His Holy Spirit that we hear only His whisper, blocking out the world's whispers. I would label the world's whispers as noise. God's gift of gentleness comes through His Holy Spirit, the same Spirit that transformed Paul and can transform us.

Before we can practice gentle self-control, humility, patience, and kindness, we must first have the anchor of God's gentle Spirit to lead the way. Paul admonished us as believers to "keep in step with the Spirit" (Galatians 5:25). The first step on this path is obeying God's command: "Be still, and know that I am God" (Psalm 46:10). We might add: *Be still and quiet.*

Stop moving. Stop talking.

Focus completely on God. Be immersed in His presence.

This is easier said than done in today's nonstop culture. Yet we can't practice gentleness without having a gentle, quiet spirit.

Seeking a Gentle and Quiet Spirit in Today's World

Pause a while and know that I am God.

Psalm 46:10 TJB

"Never be still to remember that I am God" would be our culture's revision of Psalm 46:10. The Jerusalem Bible translation is clear: *Pause a while . . . Stop . . . Take a break . . . and know that I am God.* If the Mary and Martha story of Luke 10:38–42 were retold today, Mary would be drinking coffee with Jesus, fully engaged in conversation and giving him her full and undivided attention. Martha would be trying to coordinate Jesus' appointments by making phone calls, texting, and e-mailing while being involved in a myriad of other pressing tasks. Martha would be quite proud of her stellar multitasking skills, and she would view Mary's behavior as inefficient and a waste of time, basically lazy. Luke 10:40 states that Martha was distracted.

Having "a gentle and quiet spirit" (1 Peter 3:4) was not valued any more in Jesus' day than it is today, it seems. Practicing a restrained, thoughtful spirit (taking the time to think) can be sometimes viewed as unassertive and lazy. Our country has been called the "impatient nation."[1] As a culture, we are known to be a distracted people. We are a bombarded people, a hurried people. We lead electronically interrupted lives. We become frustrated when we are denied instant gratification. Instead of gentle, quiet spirits, we suffer with agitated, stressed spirits. We live in a noisy world where retreats of silence are rarely valued.

A gentle and quiet spirit is filled with God's peace as we calm our hearts to listen to the whispers of His Spirit. It is the antithesis of an impatient, rushed, distracted, agitated, and stressed spirit. We cannot pour Christ's gentleness into the world if we allow the constant bombardment of our souls to overwhelm us.

Lest we solely blame our distraction on our digital age, we need to realize that people have been distracted since ancient times. We will see that Scripture clearly addresses this familiar issue. Thomas à Kempis wrote in the early fifteenth century: "A pure, sincere, and calm spirit is not distracted by doing many things, because it works all things to the honor of God—since it is inwardly still and quiet, it does not seek to satisfy itself in anything it does. What, indeed, hinders and troubles you more than the undisciplined desires of your own heart?"[2]

When we consider the extreme digital edges of Internet pornography, online gambling, cyber-bullying, sexting, and living in alternate virtual realities such as Second Life, it is easy to blame technology and the overload of our modern information age as the enemy. Yet technology itself is not evil any more than money, sex, or food is evil. Excessive use to the point of addiction is what destroys individuals and their relationships. An obsession with technology, sex, food, money, or anything that replaces God is the enemy of a gentle, quiet spirit. The challenge of controlling these obsessions is nothing new and has been with us since biblical times. Human beings are wired to fill their deepest needs and longings. If God is absent from our lives, we will find substitutes. God calls us to focus on a different ambition.

A DIFFERENT AMBITION

> Make it your ambition to lead a quiet life, to mind your
> own business and work with your hands, just as we told
> you, so that your daily life may win the respect of outsid-
> ers and so that you will not be dependent on anybody.
>
> 1 Thessalonians 4:11–12

Juxtaposing the words "ambition" and a "quiet life" may seem to be an oxymoron. It is another example of how following Jesus Christ turns our world's values upside down and inside out. Ambition is the strong desire to achieve success requiring determination and hard work. Our biblical calling to live a gentle, quiet, and peace-filled life is an ambitious one.

We are called to a life of peace in our souls and in our interactions with others. Romans 8:6 explains that "the mind governed by the Spirit is life and peace." First Peter 3:4 tells us that the unfading beauty of a gentle and quiet spirit in our inner self is of great worth in God's sight.

> But the wisdom that comes from heaven is first of all
> pure; then peace-loving, considerate, submissive, full of
> mercy and good fruit, impartial and sincere. Peacemak-
> ers who sow in peace raise a harvest of righteousness.
>
> James 3:17–18

Being peacemakers who sow peace in the world is an impossible task without having quiet, peaceful, gentle inner selves. Peacemakers are considerate and thoughtful, full of mercy and good fruit. Peacemakers are submissive. *Submission* is a red-flag word in our culture. Similar to gentleness, it connotes weakness and being subservient, especially for women. We must remember the object of our submission. Peacemakers are called to be submissive to God. We relinquish our control to God. We submit to the will of our Father. This determined, power-packed surrender to God's ultimate purposes is the opposite of weakness.

As much as this grates on those with an American mindset, all believers are literally called to give up.

BIBLICAL GIVING UP

We and the people there pleaded with Paul not to go up to Jerusalem. Then Paul answered, "Why are you weeping and breaking my heart? I am ready not only to be bound, but also to die in Jerusalem for the name of the Lord Jesus." When he would not be dissuaded, we *gave up* and said, "The Lord's will be done."

Acts 21:12–14

The Christians of Acts 21 were trying to protect Paul from harm, just as we would want to protect our loved ones from entering a dangerous war zone. Biblical giving up is releasing our personal desires, no matter how godly our motives appear, to say, "The Lord's will be done." We are called to align our vision with God's vision and consciously give up our will to follow His will. We trust God's ultimate purposes when we don't understand His methods. This reminds me of different missionary couples I've known who prepared for years to enter the mission field only to be prevented from traveling to a foreign country by serious illness or other barriers. They thought, *How can this be God's will?*

At the other extreme, sometimes Christians cite Psalm 37:4 to legitimize their self-absorbed "Santa Claus list" for God. I know Christians who have prayed for a new job, a new house, or nice weather for a trip. They state that when we depend on God, He will give us what we desire: "Depend on the LORD, and he will grant you your heart's desire" (Psalm 37:4 NEB).

That interpretation is backwards. God does not give us what we most desire as humans. He actually places godly desires in our hearts in line with His will. We want what God wants. That is the more miraculous gift. Throughout Scripture, we are taught to pray and seek God's guidance in accordance with His will. The verses that follow verse four in Psalm 37 clarify this for us: "Commit your life to the LORD; trust in him and he will act" (37:5 NEB); "Wait quietly for the LORD, be patient till he comes" (37:7 NEB).

Trust God . . . wait quietly . . . be patient . . . This is the core of a gentle, quiet spirit. These verses are the less exciting yet more important ones to quote about prayer from Psalm 37.

Scripture explains the connection between biblical giving up and prayer:

God assures us that He listens to us and gives us what we request if we make requests according to His will. "We can approach God with confidence for this reason: *if we make requests which accord with his will he listens to us*; and if we know that our requests are heard, we know also that the things we ask for are ours" (1 John 5:14–15 NEB).

We are accustomed to making future plans and even praying about them. Instead we should say, "If it is the Lord's will, I will do this."

> Now listen, you who say, "Today or tomorrow we will go to this or that city, spend a year there, carry on business and make money." Why, you do not even know what will

happen tomorrow. What is your life? You are a mist that appears for a little while, and then vanishes. Instead, you ought to say, "If it is the Lord's will, we will live and do this or that."

James 4:13–15

The truth is that we do not know how to pray so God's Spirit prays for us in accordance with His will. "We do not know what we ought to pray for, but the Spirit himself intercedes for us through wordless groans. And he who searches our hearts knows the mind of the Spirit, because the Spirit intercedes for God's people *in accordance with the will of God*" (Romans 8:26–27).

Aligning our vision with God's vision requires that we listen to Him. We must be on the same frequency as the Holy Spirit to listen to God's whisper.

LISTENING TO GOD'S GENTLE WHISPER

And as Elijah stood there the Lord passed by, and a mighty windstorm hit the mountain; it was such a terrible blast that the rocks were torn loose, but the Lord was not in the wind. After the wind, there was an earthquake, but the Lord was not in the earthquake. And after the earthquake, there was a fire, but the Lord was not in the fire. And after the fire, there was the sound of a *gentle whisper*. When Elijah heard it, he wrapped his face in his scarf and went out and stood at the entrance of the cave. And a voice said, "Why are you here, Elijah?"

1 Kings 19:11–13 TLB

Have you ever been on the receiving end of a discussion that escalated into a heated argument during which you were shouted at? I would imagine that the more you were shouted at, the less you listened to those angry words. That reaction is our natural coping mechanism to protect ourselves. God does not shout at us. He is not a blaring car horn demanding our attention.

In contrast, do you remember when a loving friend whispered to you in a crowded room? You probably drew yourself closer to carefully listen to those intimate, intriguing words. God's Holy Spirit is a whisperer. Philip Yancey says that God has spoken with different voices through the ages but His last voice is a soft, gentle whisper.[3] We are called to pay careful attention to God's voice (Deuteronomy 15:5). The most important part of prayer is listening to God's whispers.

Perhaps you spend time with a friend who never stops talking. You can't get a word in edgewise and when you start to speak, your friend interrupts you. He is not talking with you, but at you. This is not a mutual conversation but a one-sided lecture. Is that how God feels when His children talk at Him but do not take the time to listen to Him? When Christians explain prayer as a "continual conversation with God," do they realize that the most important part of any conversation is listening to the other speaker? "My sheep listen to my voice; I know them, and they follow me" (John 10:27).

I am grateful that God chose the written word as His chief vessel of communication. I'm glad He gave me a concrete book that explains everything He wants me to know about His character and perfect will. I had twenty-four-hour access to this information long before the digital age.

Meditation is complete immersion in God's Word and presence as we listen to Him. If meditation on God's Word sounds like a mystical experience out of your reach, Harold Chadwick explains that if you know how to obsess and worry, you know how to meditate: "Meditate upon what you have read—think deeply about it, turn it over and over in your mind. There are some who say they don't know how to meditate, but if you know how to worry, you know how to meditate."[4]

Listening to God's gentle whisper begins with quietly waiting for the Lord. This requires patience. We cannot hurry God. We are called to immerse ourselves in His Word and His presence to align our will with His will, to want what God wants. We surrender our agenda. We simply give up.

GENTLENESS AND PRAYER

The Lord is near. Do not be anxious about anything, but in every situation, by prayer and petition, with thanksgiving, present your requests to God. And the peace of God, which transcends all understanding, will guard your hearts and your minds in Christ Jesus.

Philippians 4:5–7

As we relinquish control, we understand why Paul writes, "Do not be anxious about anything, but in every situation, by prayer and petition, with thanksgiving, present your requests to God." Philippians 4:4–7 is one of the most often quoted passages about worry and prayer. Paul reassures us that we need not be concerned about anything. People filled with anxiety are not peaceful, gentle people. God's peace will guard us as we sometimes feel like we are stepping off a cliff—trusting God but wondering if our vision will remotely align with His vision.

I have heard multiple sermons based on this passage, and I've seen prayer times in church services often opened with Philippians 4:6–7 recited. But I can't remember once hearing verse five included: "Let your gentleness be evident to all. The Lord is near."

When we are gentle to all, the Lord is not just near, He is within us. We have His presence and His peace protecting us, which dwarfs any earthly problems. "Being gentle with all" is a critically important preface to prayer and seeking God's presence.

SILENT RETREATS

Great souls find peace in silence; small souls seek to be distracted by chatter and anesthetized by noise.

—David Augsburger

As I recently said good-bye to a teenager who was driving away from my home, I heard a loud noise in her car engine that warned of potential danger. When I told her that her car probably needed repair to avoid stranding her or causing an accident, she smiled and said, "It's fine. I just turn my radio on really loud and then I don't hear the noise."

We may laugh at her oblivious attitude, but too many people live by her convoluted logic. If they can fill their world with enough noisy distractions to block out any warning signs of potential danger, then they think their personal or spiritual problems won't affect them.

Quieting our souls and carving out retreat times of silence to hear God's gentle, soft voice are challenging pursuits in today's blaring world. We may not be able to travel to a mountaintop retreat, but we can take a walk during our lunch hour to pray. We can find other creative ways to refocus on God during our day. Some people give up their online activities for Lent. Others create Tech Sabbaths on one weekend a month when they abstain from all electronic communication. Yet digital input is not the only noise in the world. Even Jesus experienced difficulty in finding opportunities to listen to God's voice. He was bombarded with people constantly needing His help and searching for Him. Luke 5:16 tells us that Jesus "often withdrew to lonely places and prayed." He tried to escape the crowds for a few quiet moments until they interrupted Him again. Jesus made time to listen to God to keep himself focused on his Father's will.

At daybreak, Jesus went out to a solitary place. The people were looking for him and when they came to where he was, they tried to keep him from leaving them. But he said, "I must proclaim the good news of the kingdom of God to the other towns also, because that is why I was sent."

Luke 4:42–43

Now read Matthew 14 through your twenty-first-century eyes. I doubt you have experienced a day more stressful than this one. Even when Jesus needed to be alone after learning about the horrific murder of his second cousin, John the Baptist, the crowds followed Him. Yet in the midst of His own grief, Jesus had compassion on the crowd, healing their sick and feeding them with five loaves of bread and two fish. Few of us link the timeline of the "five loaves and two fish miracle" with John's grotesque beheading. No wonder the disciples wanted to send the crowds away as they reeled from John's death. Only after the crowd is fed does Jesus dismiss them and go up on a mountainside by himself to pray before evening comes (v. 23).

When Jesus is finally alone after a tragic and exhausting day, trying to recover in the comforting arms of His Father, then the disciples need His help in the storm! As their boat flails in the waves, Jesus does *not* rush to their aid. He does not help them until the fourth watch, 3:00–6:00 a.m. He watches them struggle all through the night. In this Matthew chapter lie two important underpinnings of our faith journey:

- The disciples are safe in Jesus' care even when they don't realize it. God is never in a hurry, because His ultimate purposes are secure.
- Our gentle Lord Jesus Christ often needed quiet recovery time with His Father in order to follow His will and minister to broken people. Why would we need any less?

Christ is born to us only through silence.

—Meister Eckhart

A Gentle, Quiet Spirit Versus Weakness

I urge, then, first of all, that petitions, prayers, intercession and thanksgiving be made for everyone—for kings and all those in authority, that we may *live peaceful and quiet lives* in all godliness and holiness. This is good, and pleases God our Savior, who wants all people to be saved and to come to a knowledge of the truth.

1 Timothy 2:1–4

Having a gentle, quiet spirit has never been more counter-cultural than it is today. Yet it is the core of being a gentle person. We are called to seek a life of peace as we listen to God's whispering voice and as we surrender our will to God's will. We may appear weak and unassertive, but what the world cannot see is that tremendous self-control and patience are required to give up our agenda for God's agenda. Our gentle, quiet spirit is built on the Rock.

In her enlightening book *Quiet: The Power of Introverts in a World That Can't Stop Talking*, Susan Cain masterfully explains the history of how extroverted, bold behaviors came to be prized and worshipped in western culture while introverted, quiet behaviors came to be viewed as passive weakness. During the 1920s the shy, reserved nature of children and adults started to receive treatment as an unwanted disease. Dynamic salesmanship became the coveted ideal, whether one was selling a vacuum, a car, or Jesus. By the 1950s anti-anxiety medications were being prescribed for quiet people to help them overcome their introverted flaws. Cain shows how this belief has become as prevalent in the evangelical church as it is in society. Talkers trump listeners, specifically loud talkers trump quiet listeners. Cain believes that "soft power is quiet persistence."[5] She dedicates her book to her grandfather, a soft-spoken rabbi who "spoke so eloquently the language of quiet."[6]

It struck me that if Jesus were executed and resurrected in our current world, every publicist and agent would be fighting over the opportunity to land Jesus as a client and organize the largest media event of the century. The announcement of Jesus' revelation would be on the level of the Super Bowl, as throngs would pack the stadium for the internationally televised event. Megachurch services would pale in comparison. Contrast this thought with the way Jesus chose to appear to His followers after He rose from the dead. He did not enter the temple or public square. He did not speak to the crowds. Jesus quietly appeared to those He loved with not one bit of fanfare. Mary thought He was the gardener. His disciples did not recognize Him. Our Lord's revelation of the most extraordinary event in all of human history was quietly whispered.

Attentiveness to the presence of God requires patient silence; the door to such solitude opens only from the inside; patient silence and solitude allow us to attune to God who is there.

—David Augsburger

A whispered echo is all that we hear of him. But who could comprehend the thunder of his power?

Job 26:14 TJB

PERSONAL RETREAT

• We are each a combination of Mary and Martha. When are you a fully engaged Mary or a distracted Martha?

• Thomas Merton, an early twentieth-century monk, said, "The greatest need of our time is to clean out the enormous mass of mental and emotional rubbish that clutters our minds." What are your current obstacles to practicing a gentle, quiet spirit and peaceful life? What rubbish clutters your mind?

• What form do your silent retreats take when you most easily hear the whispers of God? In the middle of the night? While driving in the car? During early morning walks?

• Think about how being anxious prevents us from practicing gentleness and how this affects our prayer life.

• Recite the Lord's Prayer (Matthew 6:9–13), focusing on: "Your will be done, on earth as it is in heaven." Think about seasons of your life when you gave up your agenda to align your vision with God's vision. Also think about seasons when you refused to give up your agenda and blocked out God's quiet voice.

• How often have you heard Romans 8:28 quoted to encourage others, "And we know that in all things God works for the good of those who love him…" without the end of the sentence, "who have been called according to his purpose"? Ponder that what we consider "good" or comfortable in our lives may be the antithesis of what is in accordance with God's will and His purpose (Romans 8:27–28).

Hardship is an inevitable part of life. Endure it as discipline, a sign that God is treating you as his child and is training you for holiness.

—Mark Buchanan

Everyone must choose one of two pains: the pain of discipline or the pain of regret.

—Jim Rohn

I think that somewhere along the line we feel that holiness is a gift from God that requires nothing of us—that you wake up one morning and presto! You're suddenly holy. Sorry. It takes a lot of guts, guts right down here in your stomach, and it takes a lot of effort, and a tremendous amount of grace and emptying of self to achieve holiness.

—Mother Angelica

7

PRACTICING GENTLE SELF-CONTROL

For I am the LORD your God; you shall make yourselves holy and keep yourselves holy, because I am holy.

Leviticus 11:44 NEB

Therefore, with minds that are alert and fully sober; set your hope on the grace to be brought to you when Jesus Christ is revealed at his coming. As obedient children, do not conform to the evil desires you had when you lived in ignorance. But just as he who called you is holy, so be holy in all you do; for it is written: "Be holy, because I am holy."

1 Peter 1:13–16

*T*o be holy is to be like God. Neither of the above verses states: "Feel holy." We are called to *be* holy, *make* ourselves holy, and *keep* ourselves holy. Peter gives us rock-solid advice about developing holy habits. Self-control is the key to consistently acting with gentleness and restraint. Holding our tongue and actions in check is the first step. This is a disciplined process of daily practice.

Sometimes Christians confuse justification with sanctification. Our salvation is a completed act, accomplished once and for all on the cross by Jesus Christ. We cannot earn our salvation, add to it, nor take anything away from it. Yet we are called to spend a lifetime practicing how we imitate Jesus Christ.

"For it is by grace you have been saved, through faith—and this not from yourselves, it is the gift of God—not by works, so that no one can boast. For we are God's handiwork, created in Christ Jesus to do good works, which God prepared in advance for us to do" (Ephesians 2:8–10).

Sanctification, the lifetime process of reflecting Jesus Christ, is our privilege as His followers. Paul tells us in Philippians: "Whatever happens, conduct yourselves in a manner worthy of the gospel of Christ" (1:27). We are permanent royalty, sons and daughters of the King for eternity, hence we should act in a manner worthy of our inheritance. Acting in this holy manner requires practice.

After teaching music for over thirty years, I can tell you that most people do not understand how to practice. The two most common excuses students offer to explain why they didn't practice are "I didn't have time to practice"—which translates into: "I didn't make time to practice; I spent my time other ways"—and "I didn't practice that piece because it was too hard." Would a student need to spend time practicing the piece if it were easy?

Students cannot have it both ways: the ability to play well and an easy road to make that happen. The same is true for developing any skill, including Christlike behavior. First we must make practice a priority. Then we need to realize that the more challenging a skill is, the more practice is required.

Who Needs to Practice?

Never yield to evil, practice good and you will have an everlasting home, for Yahweh loves what is right, and never deserts the devout.

Psalm 37:27–28 TJB

Behaving in a manner worthy of our faith is not a natural, automatic reaction. It is built on learned, practiced responses. It is interesting to note that the words "*practice, practical,* and *practicum*" all derive from the Greek word *praktikos,* which means "practical or concerned with action." A practical approach puts theories and ideas into practice. We all know that many wonderful ideas sound great but aren't realistic if they cannot be put into practice. Scripture teaches that we deceive ourselves when our faith is separated from taking action.

> Why do you call me, "Lord, Lord," and do not do what I say? As for everyone who comes to me and hears my words and *puts them into practice,* I will show you what they are like. They are like a man building a house, who dug down deep and laid the foundation on rock. When a flood came, the torrent struck that house but could not shake it, because it was well built. But the one who hears my words and does not put them into practice is like a man who built a house on the ground without a foundation. The moment the torrent struck that house, it collapsed and its destruction was complete.
>
> Luke 6:46–49

In biblical times, being an apprentice was well understood. Sons apprenticed with their fathers to learn their skilled craft and be mentored into the family business. Daughters were mentored by their mothers. Through a process of many years, sons and daughters daily practiced their skills, imitating their parents. They reviewed, improved, and perfected their skills into adulthood. The path to learning how to follow God was no different. This passage describes immersion throughout the day, including tangible visual reminders:

You shall take these words of mine to heart and keep them in mind; you shall bind them as a sign on the hand and wear them as a phylactery on the forehead. Teach them to your children, and speak of them indoors and out of doors, when you lie down and when you rise. Write them up on the door-posts of your houses and on your gates. Then you will live long, you and your children, in the land which the LORD swore to your forefathers to give them, for as long as the heavens are above the earth.

Deuteronomy 11:18–21 NEB

GOD CREATED OUR BRAINS

Many years of intensive deliberate practice actually change the body and the brain.

—Geoff Colvin

Learning any complex skill, which requires hours of repeated practice, changes the white matter in the brain. God designed our brains to establish neural pathways laying down tracks. You may already be familiar with the well known "10 Years or 10,000 Hours Rule." Practicing a skill with intense focus for ten years or ten thousand hours appears to be the formula for honing an expert skill. The best methods for learning any complex skill, such as playing an instrument, speaking a language, or training in a sport, always include the following:

- Daily immersion.
- Imitation of excellent models.
- Constant review and repetition.
- Challenges to stretch, grow, and improve skills.

In other words, you live and breathe this skill. It is woven throughout your day. This is the process described in Deuteronomy 11:18–21. For example, if you are learning to play an instrument, you practice in the morning, in the middle of the day, and in the evening. You are coached by a teacher who is an excellent model. When you are not practicing, you listen to high-quality recordings. You attend weekend concerts given by premiere musicians. You balance your practice time between reviewing scales, technique, and completed pieces with learning new and more difficult pieces. You stretch your skills by correcting mistakes. When you are learning a new piece, you break down sections to isolate the most difficult passages and master those separately. *You practice daily immersion.* You build natural muscle memory.

When people persevere at learning any challenging skill, a fascinating cycle occurs: The more they practice, the more natural their skills become, and the more they enjoy it. Then their pursuit becomes their passion.

If you had this experience as a child in learning an expert skill, I would imagine that at first you did not naturally know how to practice with this intense focus. Your coach, teacher, or parent guided you to develop the self-control and discipline required to learn your skill.

Now, there is nothing wrong with experiencing exposure to different fields. It is beneficial for most young people to try playing a sport, taking an art or ballet class, learning beginning pieces on an instrument, attending Sunday school, learning a few phrases of a foreign language, and being exposed to a host of other skills. We consider these people to be well-rounded. But the results between practicing immersion and exposure will be radically different. An adult who has a fluent, natural expert ability has practiced some form of immersion earlier in life. This information is important for us because what we intensely practice actually changes our brains.

BUT IS PRACTICE BIBLICAL?

It was you who created my inmost self, and put me together in my mother's womb; for all these mysteries I thank you: for the wonder of myself, for the wonder of your works. You know me through and through, from having watched my bones take shape when I was being formed in secret, knitted together in the limbo of the womb.

Psalm 139:13–15 TJB

When I study educational or psychological principles, I am amazed that God always had the idea first. But I should not be surprised. God knows exactly how we function because He is the one who created our brains.

When we are building skills and muscle memory, we are developing habits. Whether we are aware of it or not, we are laying down tracks for good or bad habits. Bad habits in extreme are addictions. We are slaves to whatever masters us (2 Peter 2:19). We daily spend our time practicing habits of behavior, whether they are positive or negative behaviors. The more we engage in a specific activity, the more ingrained and natural it becomes.

I had my first inkling about "biblical practice and muscle memory" after speaking with Kaitlyn. She was an unusually attractive Christian woman in her late twenties. Kaitlyn had received a purity ring when she was sixteen years old and signed a contract with her parents to practice abstinence until marriage. But Kaitlyn grew into a beautiful woman who was constantly being propositioned by interested, eligible men. She told me, "Sometimes I did want to have sex with these attractive men. They wanted me and I wanted them. I was no longer a teenager and my faith had waned. But it was the strangest thing. Even when I thought about giving in to temptation, I couldn't. It was sheer muscle memory. I had practiced purity and following God for so many years that I couldn't go through with a sexual affair. The self-control was ingrained in me."

Then I remembered that people who practiced sexual purity before marriage are more likely to practice sexual faithfulness to their spouses. They are not necessarily more spiritually mature people. They have the benefit of ingrained spiritual muscle memory.

Is this the application of the ten years or ten thousand hours rule?

If daily immersion practice is a biblical principle, then we need to fully understand it. If we are willing to invest years of our life to develop a respected skill, should we not be more interested in investing practice hours to imitate and follow our Lord? In Acts 17:11, we learn that the Bereans were considered of more noble character than the Thessalonians because they received the gospel with great eagerness and examined the Scriptures *every day* to see if what Paul said was true.

Paul clearly understood the immersion principle when he asked the Philippians to focus their minds on spiritual excellence and remember his example to put it into practice.

Finally, brothers and sisters, whatever is true, whatever is noble, whatever is right, whatever is pure, whatever is lovely, whatever is admirable—if anything is excellent or praiseworthy—think about such things. Whatever you have learned or received or heard from me, or seen in me—put it into practice. And the God of peace will be with you.

Philippians 4:8–9

DISCIPLINED TRAINING

We are what we repeatedly do. Excellence, then, is not an act but a habit.

—Aristotle

Training, discipline, and self-control were accepted parts of biblical culture. Paul wrote to readers who lived in the world of the Olympic Games. The games were held every four years in Olympia, Greece, during religious festivals honoring Zeus. Competing in the games was an act of worship. The ancient Greeks believed that disciplining the body and mind honored Zeus. In 1 Timothy 6:12, we read, "Fight the good fight." The Greek word *agonizomos* in this verse relates to "training for the games."

The analogy between spiritual training and physical training for athletic games in Scripture is not subtle.

Train yourself to be godly. For physical training is of some value, but godliness has value for all things, holding promise for both the present life and the life to come.

1 Timothy 4:7–8

Do you not know that in a race all the runners run, but only one gets the prize? Run in such a way as to get the prize. Everyone who competes in the games goes into strict training. They do it to get a crown of laurel that will not last, but we do it to get a crown that will last forever.

1 Corinthians 9:24–25

While several verses in Scripture mention analogies to physical training, more than two hundred verses command us to make music to God, often calling us to make excellent music, not mediocre music. Other Old Testament verses set high standards for artisans working on the temple. The disciplined training required of an apprentice learning a prized skill in biblical times should shed light on our calling. Remember that *discipline* derives from the word *disciple*. Instead of focusing on "disciplined" training, let us focus on "disciple" training. We train as we run our race toward the eternal prize of our Lord Jesus Christ with the same intensity and determination that we would pour into preparing for a twenty-six-mile marathon.

IMITATORS OF CHRIST

Spiritual maturity is necessary for imitating Christ. Imitating Christ requires us to walk as Jesus walked.

—Robert Luginbill

Paul writes in Philippians 4:8 that believers should put into practice what they have observed and learned from Paul's behavior. Paul often encourages the churches to follow his example, yet he knows that he is a flawed human being who has been mercifully rescued by God.

We were made in the image of God, intended to be His reflection (Genesis 1:26, 5:2). Then the mirror shattered and the image became unrecognizable. Jesus is the one perfect image of God who restores us to reflect our Father again. We are ultimately called to imitate God.

> To this you were called, because Christ suffered for you, leaving you an example, that you should follow in his steps.
>
> 1 Peter 2:21

> Follow God's example, therefore, as dearly loved children and walk in the way of love, just as Christ loved us and gave himself up for us as a fragrant offering and sacrifice to God.
>
> Ephesians 5:1–2

We are called to be the fragrance of Christ. If we truly imitate our Lord, our loving gentleness can be the aroma of Christ (2 Corinthians 2:15) in a hurting world. Imagine the impact we could make.

REVIEW FOR THE MIND

> Sanctify them by the truth; your word is truth. As you sent me into the world, I have sent them into the world. For them I sanctify myself, that they too may be truly sanctified. . . . I have made you known to them, and will continue

to make you known in order that the love you have for me may be in them and that I myself may be in them.

John 17:17–19, 26

Imitating Christ runs opposite of our natural behavior. God knows that we human beings need constant repetition and review. We learn through a process of immersion, but we maintain through review. We *make* ourselves holy and *keep* ourselves holy. Sanctify is the Greek word *hagiazo*, which means "to make holy." To "walk as Jesus did" requires daily practice. Paul says, "I face death every day" (1 Corinthians 15:31). He tells us to "take captive every thought to make it obedient to Christ" (2 Corinthians 10:5). Jesus explains: "Whoever wants to be my disciple must deny themselves and take up their cross *daily* and follow me" (Luke 9:23).

Paul tells us that we have the mind of Christ (1 Corinthians 2:16). Jesus claims that He is in us. But God does not wave a magic fairy wand and *POOF*—we immediately have the mind of Christ when we become His child. Developing the mind of Christ is a daily process as we let go of bad habits to replace them with holy habits:

Do not conform any longer to the pattern of this world, but be *transformed by the renewing of your mind.* Then you will be able to test and approve what God's will is—his good, pleasing and perfect will.

Romans 12:2

Do not lie to each other, since you have taken off your old self with its practices and have put on the new self, which is being *renewed in knowledge in the image of its Creator.*

Colossians 3:9–10

So *I will always remind you* of these things, even though you know them and are firmly established in the truth you now have. I think *it is right to refresh your memory* as long as I live in the tent of this body, because I know that I will soon put it aside, as our Lord Jesus Christ has made clear to me. And I will make every effort to see that after my departure *you will always be able to remember* these things.

2 Peter 1:12–15

It is not a coincidence that Peter's review process follows this advice in the preceding paragraphs: "make every effort to add to your faith goodness; and to goodness, knowledge; and to knowledge, self-control; and to self-control, perseverance; and to perseverance, godliness; and to godliness, mutual affection; and to mutual affection, love" (2 Peter 1:5–7). The facets of fruit are presented again as interconnected.

More important, Peter states that we should possess these qualities in increasing amounts, and if we claim to have knowledge of Jesus without the fruit, then we are ineffective, blind, and unproductive (2 Peter 1:8–9). We add self-control to knowledge, and perseverance, godliness, mutual affection, and love flow from those.

WHY IS SELF-CONTROL THE ANCHOR OF HEALTHY FRUIT?

Resist courageously, one habit overcomes another.

—Thomas à Kempis

Scripture teaches that self-control anchors our fruit in two main ways:

- It restrains our behaviors that do not mirror Christ.
- It prepares us to be ready and eager to do good in following our Lord. This is the gentle fight that engages us.

Restraint is the prerequisite for doing good. Several biblical passages discuss a lack of self-control in people who are drunks or quick-tempered. Having a short fuse is the opposite of gentleness. We have a God who is not quick-tempered but slow to anger (Psalm 145:8). Would a military commander send a soldier who cannot control his temper into battle? Would that commander send a soldier who is an alcoholic or a drug addict into battle? Neither soldier has the discipline to control his or her behavior. These loose cannons would probably endanger themselves on the battlefield and could never focus on the mission of their commander. God's soldiers and leaders have gentle, restrained qualities:

> Since an overseer manages God's household, he must be blameless—not overbearing, not quick-tempered, not given to drunkenness, not violent, not pursuing dishonest gain. Rather, he must be hospitable, one who loves what is good, who is self-controlled, upright, holy and disciplined.
>
> Titus 1:7–8

> Now the overseer must be above reproach, faithful to his wife, temperate, self-controlled, respectable, hospitable, able to teach, not given to drunkenness, not violent but

gentle, not quarrelsome, not a lover of money. He must manage his own family well and see that his children obey him, and he must do so in a manner worthy of full respect.

1 Timothy 3:2–4

When you read Paul's words written to Titus and Timothy, keep in mind that Paul struggled to learn to control his temper, tongue, and violent streak. In Titus 2:2–8, Paul writes that people of all ages and both genders need to learn self-control through training and following godly examples. No matter what season of life we are in, self-control is a struggle.

You, however, must teach what is appropriate to sound doctrine. Teach the *older men* to be temperate, worthy of respect, self-controlled, and sound in faith, in love and in endurance. Likewise, teach the *older women* to be reverent in the way they live, not to be slanderers or addicted to much wine, but to teach what is good. Then they can urge the *younger women* to love their husbands and children, to be self-controlled and pure, to be busy at home, to be kind, and to be subject to their husbands, so that no one will malign the word of God. Similarly, encourage the *young men* to be self-controlled. In everything set them an example by doing what is good.

Titus 2:1–7

BEING ALERT AND PREPARED

You are all children of the light and children of the day. We do not belong to the night or to the darkness. So then, let us not be like others, who are asleep, but let us be awake and sober. For those who sleep, sleep at night, and those who get drunk, get drunk at night. But since we belong to the day, let us be sober, putting on faith and love as a breastplate, and the hope of salvation as a helmet.

1 Thessalonians 5:5–8

We are called to be alert and ready to follow God on a daily basis. Yet there are added benefits for those who are self-controlled and prepared.

We want to be self-controlled so we can effectively pray. Loving others deeply will follow. We can infer that not being self-controlled can be an obstacle to prayer.

The end of all things is near. Therefore be alert and of sober mind so that you may pray. Above all, love each other deeply, because love covers over a multitude of sins.

1 Peter 4:7–8

We want to be self-controlled so we can resist the enemy of our souls and stand with others who are persevering through tough challenges to follow Christ. We can infer that not being self-controlled makes us easy prey for the enemy.

Be alert and of sober mind. Your enemy the devil prowls around like a roaring lion looking for someone to devour. Resist him, standing firm in the faith, because you know that the family of believers throughout the world is undergoing the same kind of sufferings.

1 Peter 5:8–9

We want to be self-controlled so that we can say "No" to the world's temptations, expectantly look forward to our Lord's coming, and be eager to do what is good. We can infer that not being self-controlled will ease us into saying "Yes" to temptation, cloud our focus on Jesus Christ, and prevent us from being ready to do what is good. Maybe we will be eager and ready to do what is bad.

> For the grace of God has appeared that offers salvation to all people. It teaches us to say "No" to ungodliness and worldly passions, and to live self-controlled, upright and godly lives in this present age, while we wait for the blessed hope—the appearing of the glory of our great God and Savior, Jesus Christ, who gave himself for us to redeem us from all wickedness and to purify for himself a people that are his very own, eager to do what is good.
>
> Titus 2:11–14

Paul writes to Titus that believers must learn to devote themselves to doing what is good (Titus 3:12). This is a learned process and we learn by devoting ourselves to practice.

PRACTICE SESSIONS

What makes resisting temptation difficult for many people is they don't want to discourage it completely.

—Franklin P. Jones

The next time you find yourself in a situation where your patience, self-control, gentleness, or humility is tested to the limit, ponder whether God has presented you with a practice session. Your first response in facing frustrating, tough times may be to pray, "Lord, please remove this trial from my life." Yet remember that many people may desire to play a musical instrument, excel at a sport, or master a myriad of skills, but they simply have no desire to practice for years. If we seriously want to imitate Jesus Christ, believe me, we will need to put in some intense daily practice time.

Most believers are familiar with the idea of being daily immersed in praying to God, meditating, and reading Scripture. However, these "fruit practice sessions" go beyond those disciplines of the Spirit. If you often pray, "Lord, make me more like you," then the route to your answered prayer will include multiple God-given opportunities for practice. This is the practical application of God's Word in a broken world. If you simply want healthy spiritual fruit to appear without the needed practice sessions, realize that you can't have it both ways.

Effective practice sessions for musicians and athletes always include new challenges and more difficult tasks to grow and improve their skills. Facing obstacles stretches us. In 1 Corinthians 3:1–3 and Hebrews 5:11–14, we learn that believers are called to wean off milk to consume solid food as they train and mature.

It seems logical that if we consistently practice a skill, we should be better at it tomorrow and even better next week . . . next month . . . next year . . . in thirty years. We should certainly not become worse. Have you enjoyed the privilege of knowing older people in their eighties or nineties who have lived immersed in Scripture and prayer and have been practicing following Jesus for decades or an entire lifetime? They embody Christ's kindness, gentleness, humility, patience, and other facets of fruit and truly reflect our Lord. They radiate the excitement of knowing that they will soon stand in His presence. Their lives give evidence of decades invested in practice.

In this chapter we have compared the biblical similarities between learning any expert skill and practicing gentle self-control. Yet there is one huge difference. We can usually learn our expert skills in private and hone them to a high degree before putting them on public display. But when we daily practice following Christ, everyone around us is watching. There is no rehearsal.

> Worship must involve practices of daily life that help us rehearse again and again the open, loving, sacrificial heart of our God who sees and hears the needy.
>
> —Mark Labberton

PERSONAL RETREAT

- Do you think one can practice gentleness without practicing self-control?

- Think about some of your most expert skills that drive your vocation or avocation. What was the path you followed to hone those skills? Mentally list the specific ways you daily practiced those skills through the years to reach your level of expertise.

- Now compare that path with the ways you have practiced following Jesus Christ and imitating His example. Have you made a similar investment? Have you practiced daily immersion?

- When you have faced temptations and challenges, did your biblical muscle memory kick in?

- Read 1 John 2:3–6. We know that we are in Christ when we walk as Jesus did. Reflect on how becoming a *disciple* of Jesus Christ means becoming a *disciplined* follower. Why is this daily process never completed?

- What is your most effective way to practice renewing your mind? What helps you restrain harmful behaviors so that you are prepared to do good?

- Read Ephesians 5:15–20. Paul tells us to be filled with the Spirit in place of being filled with addictions. You have read verses in this chapter that command us to be self-controlled and sober. God knows that we need to be filled up with something beyond ourselves. Think about your own addictions. Some of today's most common addictions are culturally acceptable and even respectable.

- The well-known saying "Practice makes perfect" is a myth. Practice makes our skills better, even excellent. Yet we are a work in progress. What are the current practice sessions (and who are the people) that God has brought into your life to practice imitating Him? Who helps you practice gentle restraint? Who helps you practice humility? Who helps you practice patience? Who helps you practice holding your tongue? Who helps you practice kindness?

Humility is not thinking less of yourself, it's thinking of yourself less.

—C. S. Lewis

The more humble we are in ourselves, and the more subject we are to God, the more prudent we will be in our affairs, and the more we will enjoy peace and quiet in our hearts.

—Thomas à Kempis

Pride fuels judgmental attitudes. Arrogance is perhaps the most socially acceptable form of sin in the church today. In this culture of abundance, one of the only ways Satan can keep Christians neutralized is to wrap us up in pride. Conceit slips in like drafts of cold air in the winter.

—David Kinnaman

8

PRACTICING GENTLE HUMILITY

Finally, all of you, be like-minded, be sympathetic, love one another, be compassionate and humble. Do not repay evil with evil or insult with insult. On the contrary, repay evil with blessing, because to this you were called so that you may inherit a blessing.

1 Peter 3:8–9

A gentle person has a humble attitude that leads to patient actions. As with all of the "softer" fruit, you cannot practice one characteristic without practicing the other. Think back to your grade school days when certain students always cut in line to be first. Their message was, "I am more important than you are. My time is more valuable than your time." Since then you have probably experienced similar dismissal in countless ways as an adult—standing in supermarket lines or driving on the road to being passed over for a promotion at work.

Graciously waiting and not calling attention to ourselves are seen as signs of weakness in our culture. Contrast this with our culture's craving for publicity, fame, and "shining a spotlight on me." We live in a competitive world that worships winners. We are rewarded for proudly asserting ourselves. Demanding attention may bring worldly visibility and success, but it does not wear the clothing of Christ. We are called to seek God through obeying Him as we seek humility and integrity (Zephaniah 2:3).

During one vacation, my husband stood in a long line in a bank. A high-profile political figure, known for her stand on helping the less fortunate, entered the bank. To everyone's surprise, this champion of the downtrodden walked straight to the front of the line, ignoring the people who were waiting. I wonder if we Christians sometimes appear to do the same. We espouse defending the helpless but our daily actions communicate a complete lack of humility and patience. We are products of our culture.

Throughout the gospels, Jesus states that "the last will be first, and the first will be last."

> People will come from east and west and north and south, and will take their places at the feast in the king- dom of God. Indeed there are those who are last who will be first, and first who will be last.
>
> Luke 13:29–30

Jesus' words also apply to current-day Pharisees. God calls us to practice humility. We stand at the back of the line in life. We may appear weak and unassertive, but we understand the strength required to practice restraint.

HUMILITY DEFINED

One of the best definitions of humility is found in Philip- pians 2:3–8 where Paul writes:

> Do nothing out of selfish ambition or vain conceit. Rather, in humility value others above yourselves, not looking to your own interests but each of you to the interests of the

others. In your relationship with one another, have the mindset as Christ Jesus: Who, being in very nature God, did not consider equality with God something to be used to his own advantage; rather, he made himself nothing by taking the very nature of a servant, being made in human likeness. And being found in appearance as a man, he humbled himself by becoming obedient to death—even death on a cross!

Paul is not asking us to die on the cross. He is asking us to have the same attitude as our Savior who did. Other translations of Philippians 2:5 call us to have the "mind of Christ."

We practice humility when we

- eliminate selfish ambition and vain conceit from our lives.
- consider others better than ourselves.
- look to the interests of others.
- become servants.

The greatest among you will be your servant. For those who exalt themselves will be humbled, and those who humble themselves will be exalted.

Matthew 23:11–12

CONSIDERATE HUMILITY TO ALL

Remind the people to be subject to rulers and authorities, to be obedient, to be ready to do whatever is good, to slander no one, to be peaceable and considerate, and always to be gentle toward everyone.

Titus 3:1–2

We are called to be gentle, peaceful, and considerate, and to show humility toward *all* people. Then why do Christians sometimes appear arrogant and rude to unbelievers as well as other believers? We often seem to have all the answers and refuse to consider alternate points of view. Too often we give the impression that *we* are the doctor, instead of pointing *to* the doctor, our Great Physician. We can only offer a heartfelt referral. We forget that we are hospital patients lying in the next bed, recovering from multiple major surgeries as our physician sets our brokenness, cleans out the cancer in our soul, and heals our wounds. Christians should be the most humble people, understanding the extreme measures taken by our doctor to rescue us when we were on our deathbed. Thomas à Kempis wrote, "We are all frail, but you should think of no one as being frailer than yourself."

Our Enemy, Pride

Human pride is the enemy of humility. Warnings about succumbing to pride are woven throughout Proverbs.

A man's pride brings him humiliation, he who humbles himself will win honor.

29:23 TJB

Pride comes before disaster, and arrogance before a fall. Better sit humbly with those in need than divide the spoil with the proud.

16:18–19 NEB

The fear of the LORD is a training in wisdom, and the way to honour is humility.

15:33 NEB

In Colossians 2:18–23, Paul confronts false humility, which is taking sick pride in appearing humble, wise, and spiritual. You may be familiar with the joke about a man who went to church and left the service, thinking, "I was the most humble person there." Acting humble is radically different from truly knowing how broken and undeserving we are. Humility is not a behavior; it is a realization.

God tells us: "But my eyes are drawn to the man of humbled and contrite spirit, who trembles at my word" (Isaiah 66:2 TJB). In other words, you may fool other people but you can't fool God. Scripture bears out this truth in God's consistent selection of the least qualified and most humble candidates to accomplish His purposes, starting with Moses.

MEEK MOSES

Moses is described in Number 12:3 as "the most humble of men, the humblest man on earth" (TJB). In our eyes, Moses affirms his meekness when he pleads with God to send someone else to speak to His people because Moses feels deficient: "never in my life have I been a man of eloquence, either before or since you have spoken to your servant. I am a slow speaker and not able to speak well" (Exodus 4:10–11 TJB). God is angry with Moses and decides to use Aaron, his brother who is a capable speaker, as Moses' mouthpiece. God does not let Moses off the hook. Moses will speak through Aaron, as God instructs Moses.

Do you ever wonder if Moses was truly meek, or was he a coward? Was he genuinely humble, or was he fearful? Now read the second chapter of Exodus. This "meek" man who was raised in Pharaoh's household was a murderer. As a young man, Moses killed an Egyptian for striking a Hebrew and hid him in the sand, making sure that no one saw him (2:13). Then when Moses realized that others discovered his crime, he escaped to the land of Midian. Several years passed before God appeared to him in the burning bush, after Moses had married, fathered a son, and shepherded his father-in-law's flocks in the wilderness. Perhaps Moses was no less humble than Paul was before God transformed him.

THE LIFESTYLE OF HUMILITY

Peter encourages us to embrace humility as a lifestyle as he quotes Proverbs 3:34:

Clothe yourselves in humility toward one another, because, "God opposes the proud but shows favor to the humble." Humble yourselves, therefore, under God's mighty hand, that he may lift you up in due time. Cast all your anxiety on him because he cares for you.

1 Peter 5:5–7

How often have you heard 1 Peter 5:7 quoted when you or another believer is worried about challenging struggles? We are quick to offer the isolated verse as comfort: "Cast all your anxiety on him because he cares for you." Peter writes chapter 5 to elder leaders and young men, but the message applies to all our lives. We are not called to simply clothe ourselves in humility but to clothe ourselves in humility *toward one another.* That's the hard part. The critical message of this passage is that when we truly humble ourselves and put others first, we naturally tend to feel anxious and worry. If we don't take care of our own interests, who will? This is the anxiety we are called to give to God, knowing that we are not forgotten. He will lift us up in due time. "Humble yourselves before the Lord, and he will lift you up" (James 4:10).

While the book of Proverbs warns us about the dangers of pride, the Psalms proclaim God's deliverance of the humble. When we humble ourselves before God, we can trust that He will hold us up, listen to us, strengthen us, guide and instruct us, and give us lasting reward.

> Yahweh, you listen to the wants of the humble, you bring strength to their hearts, you grant them a hearing . . .
>
> Psalm 10:17 TJB

> Our Lord is great, all-powerful, of infinite understanding. Yahweh, who lifts up the humble, humbles the wicked to the ground.
>
> Psalm 147:5-6 TJB

> Yahweh is so good, so upright, he teaches the way to sinners; in all that is right he guides the humble, and instructs the poor in his way.
>
> Psalm 25:8–9 TJB

> A little longer, and the wicked will be no more, search his place well, he will not be there; but the humble shall have the land for their own to enjoy untroubled peace.
>
> Psalm 37:10–11 TJB

HUMBLE LIKE LITTLE CHILDREN

> Jesus said, "Let the little children come to me, and do not hinder them, for the kingdom of heaven belongs to such as these."
>
> Matthew 19:14

Throughout the Old and New Testaments, God asks us to approach Him with the humility of young children. Jesus taught that they are our best models. In Matthew 11:25–26, Jesus explains that God hid His truth from the wise and learned and revealed it to little children. Young children had the least amount of power in biblical culture versus our Western child-centered culture of today. A young child was the least important person in the room. You can imagine the incredulous reaction of adult listeners upon hearing Jesus' teachings, which sounded like nonsense.

> At that time the disciples came to Jesus and asked, "Who, then, is the greatest in the kingdom of heaven?" He called a little child to him, and placed the child among them. And he said: "Truly, I tell you, unless you change and become like little children, you will never enter the kingdom of heaven. Therefore, whoever takes the lowly position of this child is the greatest in the kingdom of heaven. And whoever welcomes one such child in my name welcomes me."
>
> Matthew 18:1–5

While Jesus compares true followers of God to young children, Old Testament passages describe our relationship with God as helpless infants trusting their parents.

> At her breast will her nurslings be carried and fondled in her lap. Like a son comforted by his mother will I comfort you.
>
> Isaiah 66:12–13 TJB

Yahweh, my heart has no lofty ambitions, my eyes do not look too high. I am not concerned with great affairs or marvels beyond my scope. Enough for me to keep my soul tranquil and quiet like a child in its mother's arms, as content as a child that has been weaned. Israel, rely on Yahweh, now and for always!

Psalm 131 TJB

Infants and young children trust their parents and caretakers without reservation. The kingdom of God belongs to those who trust God with the same unquestioning dependence.

JESUS AS HUMBLE SERVANT

The spirit of the LORD GOD is upon me because the LORD has anointed me; he has sent me to bring good news to the humble, to bind up the broken-hearted, to proclaim liberty to captives and release to those in prison.

Isaiah 61:1 NEB

Now we come to the most astonishing portrayal of humility in Scripture. Jesus did not simply provide us with an *example* of humility. He was the *essence* of humility. We are amazed that Jesus knew He was the Son of God when He allowed His enemies to treat Him with disdain and torment Him. He completely emptied himself unto death to rescue broken, humbled, and invisible people through His humility. There was no other way.

We had all gone astray like sheep, each taking his own way, and Yahweh burdened him with the sins of all of us. Harshly dealt with, he bore it humbly, he never opened his mouth, like a lamb that is led to the slaughterhouse, like a sheep that is dumb before its shearers never opening its mouth.

Isaiah 53:6–7 TJB

Throughout Scripture, we read about Jesus' humble life. But *humble* is too kind a word. Viewing Jesus' life through the lens of our culture, we observe that he lived a *humiliated* life (from the Latin word *humiliate*, which means to "make humble"). Though our culture does not reward humility, this trait can still be viewed as a positive though weak characteristic. But humiliation? That connotes sheer embarrassment and shame. When we see people who have been humiliated and brought down, we often blame them for bringing it upon themselves. Who would choose to be humiliated? Certainly not a king.

See now, your king comes to you; he is victorious, he is triumphant, humble and riding on a donkey, on a colt, the foal of a donkey.

Zechariah 9:9 TJB

In his humiliation he was deprived of justice. Who can speak of his descendants? For his life was taken from the earth.

Acts 8:33 (Isaiah 53:8)

The evening meal was in progress, and the devil had already prompted Judas, the son of Simon Iscariot, to betray Jesus. Jesus knew that the Father had put all things under his power, and that he had come from God and was returning to God, so he got up from the meal, took off his outer clothing, and wrapped a towel around his waist. After that, he poured water into a basin and began to wash his disciples' feet, drying them with the towel that was wrapped around him.

John 13:2–5

Jesus as God incarnate put himself in humiliating circumstances. He washed people's feet, even the feet of the man who betrayed Him. He rode on a donkey. He was mocked, beaten, and killed in the cruelest of methods reserved for common criminals. He went to his death without complaining or defending himself. These facts are the meat of the gospel, but sometimes we sweep away the other humiliations that Jesus endured. He came into this world with *nothing*. The status of having family wealth, land ownership, powerful position, or beauty were just as important in the biblical world as they are today. God chose to come as a baby without any of those trappings.

Beauty was prized in Roman culture with the same intensity that it is worshipped in our culture. Our gaze and attention have always been drawn to attractive people since the beginning of civilization. Beauty equals power. This message is so engrained in us that when most people feel God's presence and envision Jesus with them, they do not imagine an ugly Jesus. Now read Isaiah 53:2–5 (TJB), which explains in detail the ultimate humiliation of our Lord:

Like a sapling he grew up in front of us, like a root in arid ground. Without beauty, without majesty (we saw him), no looks to attract our eyes; a thing despised and rejected by men, a man of sorrows and familiar with suffering, a man to make people screen their faces; he was despised

119

and we took no account of him. And yet ours were the sufferings he bore, ours the sorrows he carried. But we, we thought of him as someone punished, struck by God, and brought low. Yet he was pierced through for our faults, crushed for our sins. On him lies a punishment that brings us peace, and through his wounds we are healed.

HUMILIATED JESUS

From His birth to His death, Jesus lived with not one bit of status that human beings value or draws their attention. Isaiah 53:2–7 makes it clear that Jesus

- was unattractive.
- was ignored and treated as invisible.
- was blamed for His suffering and being punished by God.
- silently endured His death, the epitome of weakness.

The Isaiah verses become more powerful as we read 1 Samuel 16:6–7 (TJB): "Surely Yahweh's anointed one stands there before him," but Yahweh said to Samuel, "Take no notice of his appearance or his height for I have rejected him; God does not see as man sees; man looks at appearances but Yahweh looks at the heart."

Our culture's view of Jesus would be as laughable as in biblical culture. Appearance is the first thing we notice. Worldly position and wealth are close seconds. We are taught that first impressions are critical. "You cannot tell a book by its cover" is no longer a popular saying. If we are not born beautiful, we are encouraged to spend much of our resources of time and money on becoming as attractive as possible. The goal is to receive desired attention and never be ignored. Humility, a lack of importance, is anathema in a world of entitlement that focuses on building self-esteem. God does not see the outward accouterments of life. He only sees our hearts.

When we read Luke 14:7–11, we realize that Jesus is not simply giving advice about humility. He is living it.

> When he noticed how the guests picked the places of honor at the table, he told them this parable: "When someone invites you to a wedding feast, do not take the place of honor, for a person more distinguished than you may have been invited. If so, the host who invited both of you will come, and say to you, 'Give this person your seat.' Then, *humiliated*, you will have to take the least important place. But when you are invited, take the lowest place, so that when your host comes, he will say to you, 'Friend, move up to a better place.' Then you will be honored in the presence of all the other guests. For all those who exalt themselves will be humbled, and those who humble themselves will be exalted."

Jesus' entire life was an example of humility and restraint, showing us how to empty ourselves to serve others. Facing His crucifixion, Jesus washed the disciples' feet, including Judas' feet. He told His disciples, "I have set you an example that you should do as I have done for you" (John 13:14). Jesus said that a servant is not greater than his master (John 13:16). There are few subservient tasks as lowly as washing someone's dirty feet. Most people could tolerate washing a close friend's feet but would feel humiliated to wash the feet of an enemy who plotted their execution. Jesus followed the path of humiliation all the way to the cross.

Humility is the only fitting attitude for creatures who are on their way to the fullness of God's kingdom. To be sure, there is also room for prophetic critique in our struggles with the crucial issues of modern life. But those corrective words must be spoken humbly, for we ourselves have fled to the cross for healing and correction—and, having experienced there some measure of repair, are emboldened to point others to the Source of the tender mercies that have touched our lives.

—Richard Mouw

PERSONAL RETREAT

- How do you define humility in your life? Ponder that humility is not a behavior, but a realization.

- Does it make you feel anxious to practice humility toward other people, genuinely putting their interests above your interests or your family's interests?

- When have you experienced completely trusting God like a young child?

- Have you ever viewed a painting or movie that depicts an unattractive Jesus? Reflect on our Lord's entrance into this world without one bit of human status and His intent to endure humiliation on all fronts.

- Have you ever served another human being in a way that others viewed as humiliating for you? When have you followed Jesus' example of emptying yourself of pride?

How will your patience gain a crown if you have no adversity to test you?

—Thomas à Kempis

Those who love their own noise are impatient of everything else.

—Thomas Merton

Hope that is seen is no hope at all. Who hopes for what he already has? But if we hope for what we do not yet have, we wait for it patiently. In the same way, the Spirit helps us in our weakness. We do not know what we ought to pray for, but the Spirit himself intercedes for us through wordless groans. And he who searches our hearts knows the mind of the Spirit, because the Spirit intercedes for God's people in accordance with the will of God.

Romans 8:24–27

9

PRACTICING GENTLE PATIENCE

As a prisoner for the Lord, then, I urge you to live a life worthy of the calling you have received. Be completely humble and gentle; be patient, bearing with one another in love. Make every effort to keep the unity of the Spirit through the bond of peace.

Ephesians 4:1–3

Be gentle, humble, and patient. Paul mentions these three qualities in the same breath in letters written to the Ephesians, the Corinthians, and the Colossians. Patience is the practical application of gentleness that the world observes. You may consider yourself a gentle, humble person, but if you are impatient with others, what will people remember about you?

When John, a partner with a high-powered corporate firm, learned about the topic of this book project, he commented, "That sounds great on paper. But anyone with those gentle, patient, humble qualities wouldn't last twenty-four hours in most companies." John's sense of humor came through when he later e-mailed me "Murphy's Lesser Known Laws." Law number 7 is "The things that come to those who wait will be the things left by those who got there first."

You may laugh at law number 7, but you probably wonder on a bad day if getting stuck with life's leftovers because you practiced patience is a price you are willing to pay.

In contrast to our culture, Scripture calls us to practice patience and perseverance in the routine of our daily lives as well as throughout a lifetime. To avoid confusion, we will refer to perseverance as long-haul patience. Sometimes we wait for weeks, months, years, decades, or an entire life for God to lift us up, though He always carries us. For many of us, our greatest challenges and burdens will only be lifted in eternity.

Patience is the bedrock of the Christian life. Practicing patience in the face of adversity chisels our character, which leads to hope in Christ that never disappoints. God tells us that waiting will be worth it.

> We also glory in our sufferings, because we know that suffering produces perseverance; perseverance, character; and character, hope. And hope does not put us to shame, because God's love has been poured out into our hearts through the Holy Spirit, who has been given to us.
>
> Romans 5:3–5

LONG-HAUL PATIENCE: HOLDING STEADY

> Consider it pure joy, my brothers and sisters, whenever you face trials of many kinds, because you know that the testing of your faith produces perseverance. Let perseverance finish its work so that you may be mature and complete, not lacking anything.
>
> James 1:2–4

Long-haul patience, being faithful to God no matter our earthly circumstances, is one of the most powerful ways to develop mature character and the mind of Christ. We are called to "run with perseverance the race marked out for us" (Hebrews 12:1). Throughout the book of Revelation, churches are commended for "persevering" or "patiently enduring." John establishes himself in Revelation 1 as "John, your brother and companion in the suffering and kingdom and patient endurance that are ours in Jesus" (1:9). Long-haul patience is a key theme in our redemptive story.

Our "impatient nation" does not find patient waiting very exciting. Quietly holding steady is not the meat of an action movie. If there is a trait that our culture values less than weakness, it is inaction. Staying the course when we could easily take matters into our own hands to improve our situation seems like a poor approach to leading a successful life. Staying the course means following God's Word when the world says, "There is an easier way." Our inaction appears foolish.

A few years ago I wrote *Living with Thorns* in an attempt to biblically wrestle with my own thorns and understand why God did not remove the thorns of many people I cared about. Since its publication I have received numerous letters from readers who live with physical, relational, emotional, mental, or spiritual thorns. They patiently follow God in the midst of their suffering, trusting His ultimate purpose in their lives. Like Paul, they have prayed for years that God would remove their pain and now understand that God embraces them as He whispers, "Wait." They have come to realize that patiently enduring their thorns is the key to developing spiritual maturity. Our deepest wounds and most private pain will only be healed in eternity when we are enveloped by Jesus' arms.

DAILY PATIENCE

> Live in peace with each other. And we urge you, brothers and sisters, warn those who are idle and disruptive,

encourage the disheartened, help the weak, be patient with *everyone*.

1 Thessalonians 5:12–14

It is one thing to wait patiently for God's intervening hand in our lives, trusting that our Father is molding our spiritual character, yet it is quite another to wait patiently *on other people* in the midst of our daily routine. Just as we are called to be gentle with all people, we are called to be patient with everyone. We do not have the luxury of being irritated or in a hurry with our family members, coworkers, clients, students, customers, strangers, or anyone who crosses our path. Sometimes practicing daily patience is more difficult than patiently accepting God's path for one's life. Quietly enduring the small daily irritations of life when we are ignored or treated rudely is often the bigger challenge. Responding to those irritations with gentleness and kindness seems too much to ask.

No one in Scripture understands our frustration better than Paul. "Christ Jesus came into the world to save sinners—of whom I am the worst. But for that very reason I was shown mercy so that in me, the worst of sinners, Christ Jesus might display his unlimited patience as an example for those who would believe in him and receive eternal life" (1 Timothy 1:15–16).

Remember that Paul was arrogant, impatient, angry, intolerant, and violent before God transformed him. He described himself as a "blasphemer and a persecutor and a violent man" (1 Timothy 1:13). He rightfully considered himself the "worst of sinners." Yet, he is the best example of Christ's display of unlimited patience. When Paul calls us to imitate Jesus' limitless patience, he has been a recipient of that mercy. He also tells us in Romans 2:4 that God's kindness, tolerance, and patience are intended to lead to our repentance. Christ's example is the reason we can strive for daily patience.

Paul makes it clear that we are called to mirror Christ in the worst of circumstances. Why would we need to be reminded to be gentle, kind, patient, and loving when life is easy? Paul is specific in listing his hardships lest anyone discredit his sufferings as less painful than theirs. Note how he does not differentiate between the two. Suffering and being Christlike are an intertwined experience: "as servants of God we commend ourselves in every way: in great endurance; in troubles, hardships and distresses; in beatings, imprisonments and riots; in hard work, sleepless nights and hunger; in purity, understanding, patience and kindness; in the Holy Spirit and in sincere love" (2 Corinthians 6:4–6).

> You, however, know all about my teaching, my way of life, my purpose, faith, patience, love, endurance, persecutions, sufferings—what kinds of things happened to me in Antioch, Iconium and Lystra, the persecutions I endured. Yet the Lord rescued me from all of them. In fact, everyone who wants to live a godly life in Christ Jesus will be persecuted.
>
> 2 Timothy 3:10–12

We may not be beaten, imprisoned, starved, sleep deprived, or persecuted as Paul was, but we can relate to being patient, kind, and loving in difficult circumstances or with difficult people when we least want to extend that behavior.

Patience is the result of well-centered strength;
it takes the strength of Almighty God to keep a
man patient.

—Oswald Chambers

PAUL LEARNS PATIENCE

Now read my favorite example of Paul's patience in Acts
16:22–35, which puts any struggles I have with practicing
patience to shame. Paul definitely practiced what he preached.

The crowd joined in the attack against Paul and Silas, and
the magistrates ordered them to be stripped and beaten.
After they had been severely flogged, they were thrown
into prison, and the jailer was commanded to guard them
carefully. Upon receiving such orders, he put them in the
inner cell and fastened their feet in the stocks.

About midnight Paul and Silas were praying and
singing hymns to God, and the other prisoners were listening to them. Suddenly there was such a violent earthquake that the foundations of the prison were shaken.
At once all the prison doors flew open, and everybody's
chains came loose. The jailer woke up, and when he saw
the prison doors open, he drew his sword and was about
to kill himself because he thought the prisoners had
escaped. But Paul shouted, "Don't harm yourself! We are
all here!"

The jailer called for lights, rushed in, and fell trembling before Paul and Silas. He then brought them out and asked, "Sirs, what must I do to be saved?"

They replied, "Believe in the Lord Jesus, and you will be saved—you and your household." Then they spoke the word of the Lord to him and to all the others in his house. At that hour of the night the jailer took them and washed their wounds; then immediately he and all his family were baptized. The jailer brought them into his house and set a meal before them, and the whole family was filled with joy, because they had come to believe in God.

When it was daylight, the magistrates sent their officers to the jailer with the order: "Release those men."

To experience the full impact of Paul's experience in Acts 16 would require being shielded from the end of the story. In hindsight we immediately jump to the miraculous outcomes. The jailer and all of his household were saved. They washed the wounds of Paul and Silas and spread a meal before them, probably a celebratory feast. Then Paul and Silas were released from prison. But that is not where this story started. And in our own lives, we also cannot see the end of the story when we are trying to remain faithful to God in excruciating circumstances.

Imagine that you and someone you love have been

- stripped,
- severely beaten,
- thrown in prison,
- put in a cell with no air or light, and
- fastened in stocks to ensure that you cannot escape.

Then the miracle of all miracles happens. As you are worshiping and trusting God, He sends an earthquake to free you. This is the best action movie script ever written. God has literally broken your chains and opened your prison door.

And you don't leave?

Isn't it obvious that God has miraculously engineered your escape against all odds? Isn't it clear that He has not only saved you but also made a way to lead the other prisoners to freedom? You are the hero of this action movie.

And you do . . . nothing? Are you crazy? Are you stupid?

But Paul patiently waited.

Paul, the man of action, stayed put. He certainly didn't know what he was waiting for. Like us, he understood God's bigger miracle and purpose only in hindsight.

How often do we not reach the end of the story because we didn't patiently wait and endure? Was it a bad marriage? Was it a cruel parent that we cut off communication with? Was it an adult child on drugs who pushed us too far? Was it a boss who didn't appreciate us? Was it a friend who betrayed us?

Luke tells us in Acts that the other prisoners were listening and watching. When Paul and Silas stayed put, the prisoners followed their example.

Remember. The world is watching us.

When Paul tells us to not become weary in doing good, he means it. He encourages us to not give up, especially when we do not know the end of the story. God calls us to trust Him as we practice gentleness toward others and patiently wait.

Let us not become weary in doing good, for at the proper time we will reap a harvest if we do not give up. Therefore, as we have opportunity, let us do good to all people, especially to those who belong to the family of believers.

Galatians 6:9–10

God is seldom instantaneous about doing the most significant things.

—Mark Labberton

Personal Retreat

- You may know the term *grit* as "patient perseverance and resolved determination," as when someone "grits" his teeth. Grit reveals strength of character. What is the balance in our lives between practicing long-haul patience and godly giving up? What is biblical grit?

- Read James 5:7–11. James calls us to be an example of patience in the face of suffering, inspired by Job's perseverance. He tells us not to grumble against each other. James reminds us that God is full of compassion and mercy. In reality, how can we patiently suffer without complaining and trust that God is compassionate and merciful? We may restrain from grumbling if our trial lasts for a few hours or days, but how do we endure if we face trials that last for months, years, or a lifetime?

- Read Paul's prayer for the Colossian people in Colossians 1:10–12. Think about how our reliance on God's strength to patiently endure any challenging circumstances pleases our Father.

- God is never in a rush. Jesus did not hurry when Lazarus became sick. After Lazarus' death, Martha and Mary each challenged Jesus, "Lord, if you had been here, my brother would not have died" (John 11: 21, 32). Think about passages in Scripture when God was not in a hurry, and then think about experiences in your own life when God did not rush. Like Martha and Mary, you wondered, "Why are you delaying, Lord?" In hindsight, was there value in patiently waiting?

- Are you currently in the midst of a waiting period, not knowing the end of the story?

The gentle words of the wise are heard above the shouts of a king of fools.

Ecclesiastes 9:17 TJB

Yahweh, you examine me and know me,
    you know if I am standing or sitting,
    you read my thoughts from far away,
    whether I walk or lie down, you are watching,
    you know every detail of my conduct.
The word is not even on my tongue,
    Yahweh, before you know all about it;
    close behind and close in front you fence me
        around,
    shielding me with your hand.
Such knowledge is beyond my understanding,
    a height to which my mind cannot attain.

Psalm 139:1–6 TJB

PRACTICING GENTLE COMMUNICATION

For the kingdom of God is not a matter of talk but of power. What do you prefer? Shall I come to you with a rod of discipline, or shall I come in love and with a gentle spirit?

1 Corinthians 4:20–21

"*A*ctions speak louder than words."

"Talk is cheap."

We espouse these familiar sayings in defense of our actions, but the truth is that harsh, unkind words can sabotage the best actions. Mark Labberton observes, "Sticks and stones may break our bones, but words can tear our heart out."[1] The most important way we communicate gentleness to the world is through our speech.

Psalm 139 tells us that God knows all our thoughts, actions, and words before we speak them. Those three revealers of the soul are consistent in genuine, authentic people. These people do not say one thing and do another, which is the definition of hypocrisy. Their words do not undermine their actions. They realize that godly actions and words begin with godly thoughts.

Words are clothes that thoughts wear.

—Samuel Butler

SPEECH REVEALS OUR HEART

The heart of the righteous contemplates kind actions, the mouth of wicked men spews out malice.

Proverbs 15:28

How can we plan acts of kindness if we are spewing malice from our lips? The reason our choice of words is critically important is that those words reveal our true heart condition.

Don't you see that whatever enters the mouth goes into the stomach and then out of the body? But the things that come out of a person's mouth come from the heart, and these defile them.

Matthew 15:17–18

The gospels teach us that a tree is recognized by its good or bad fruit (Matthew 12:33–37 and Luke 6:43–45). The words that leave our mouth are the best indication of our spiritual fruit.

Make a tree good and its fruit will be good, or make a tree bad and its fruit will be bad, for a tree is recognized by its fruit. You brood of vipers, how can you who are evil say anything good? For the mouth speaks what the heart is full of.

Matthew 12:33–34

What Gentle Speech Is *Not*

The Bible offers us a comprehensive course on Christlike, gentle communication. Think of this chapter as a crash course. This section will first focus on what is *not* godly speech. You will find no surprises here. We do not practice godly gentle speech when we

- *Argue and provoke quarrels.* Proverbs 18:6; Philippians 2:14–15; 1 Timothy 6:3–5; 2 Timothy 2:23–25.
- *Stir up controversies.* 1 Timothy 1:5–6; 2 Timothy 2: 14–16.
- *Gossip.* Proverbs 12:18; 16:27–28.
- *Are idle busybodies.* 1 Timothy 5:13; 2 Thessalonians 3:11.
- *Betray confidences.* Proverbs 11:13; 20:19; 25:9–10.
- *Slander, when lies and gossip turn vicious.* Participating in slander includes listening to slander. Proverbs 10:18; 17:4; James 4:11.
- *Use profanity or coarse language.* Ephesians 5:4; Colossians 3:8; James 3:8–10.
- *Nag and pester.* Proverbs 19:13; 25:24.
- *Criticize and find fault.* Proverbs 10:12; 19:11.
- *Unleash our temper and impatience.* Proverbs 14:29; 15:18; 29:11; 29:22.

Ruins of Careless Speech

Through his mouth the godless man is the ruin of his neighbor, but by knowledge the virtuous are safeguarded.

Proverbs 11:9 TJB

As you read the above list of behaviors, you probably thought, "That's not a very nice person." Perhaps you know people who embody the opposite of gentle speech and behavior. They display a bad temper, frequently argue, incite conflict, curse, and attack the reputations of others. Or they gossip, nag, betray confidences, are critical, or insert themselves in other people's business. They could be your coworkers, neighbors, church members, relatives, or acquaintances. You might not shun them, but I doubt you include them in your circle of intimates—those people you most trust and respect. You would not feel safe with them and would naturally put up walls to protect yourself from them. The only thing worse than interfacing with a difficult and unloving person is actually being this person.

Note why Scripture advises us to avoid being close friends with angry people: "Make friends with no man who gives way to anger, make no hasty-tempered man a companion of yours, for fear you learn from his behavior and in this risk the loss of your own life" (Proverbs 22:24–25 TJB).

Scripture does not tell us to avoid associating with angry people. It cautions us to not make them our close companions and models. If Scripture commanded us to not associate with angry people or anyone who practices ungodly behaviors, we would need to live as hermits. Also, remember that each one of us is like Paul, the "worst of sinners." We would live equally lonely lives. God calls us to gently love hurting, broken people but not model their behavior. This requires acute awareness of our own weaknesses.

Psalm 34 offers us the best summary of practicing godly speech: "Malice must be banished from your tongue, deceitful conversation from your lips; never yield to evil, practice good, seek peace, pursue it" (Psalm 34:13–14 TJB). We must banish malice and destructive conservation from our lips to practice good and pursue peace. Malice and peace cannot coexist. Now that we know what not to do when we open our mouths, let's look at what we can do to practice gentle speech. The most effective way to curtail a destructive habit is to replace it with a constructive habit.

SPEAKING AS GOD SPEAKS

> If anyone speaks, they should do so as one who speaks the very words of God.
>
> 1 Peter 4:11

In 2 Corinthians Paul echoes Peter's words: "in Christ we speak before God with sincerity, like those sent from God" (2:17). When we dare to speak, we must realize that we are speaking as God's messengers. Note that Peter writes "if" anyone speaks, not "when." We will see that in situations where we cannot speak as Christ would speak, it is far better not to open our mouths. We may not contribute to ease a difficult situation, but at least we will not cause more damage.

Scripture teaches that God's Spirit speaks through us (Matthew 10:19–20), but first we must be aligned with His Spirit and listening to Him. Our minds guide our speech: "The wise man's mind guides his speech, and what his lips impart increases learning" (Proverbs 16:23 NEB). If we do not have the mind of Christ, our words will reveal that. Jesus was the master of thoughtfully speaking wise, kind words to hurting people.

Psalm 37:30–31 tells us that "how we talk, we walk." "The mouths of the righteous utter wisdom, and their tongues speak what is just. The law of their God in their hearts; their feet do not slip."

What Godly Speech Is

There are some whose thoughtless words pierce like a sword, but the tongue of the wise brings healing.

Proverbs 12:18 TJB

We are called to choose our words carefully. Gentle speech is restrained, thoughtful speech. Psalm 64:3–4 describes wicked men who use their sharp tongues like swords and their bitter words like arrows, shot at innocent people without warning. Those are snipers. Instead of being verbal hit men, we want to be the extreme opposite, verbal healers. Think of your words as tools that God can use to soothe and heal broken hearts and spirits. But good intentions often fail. How can we accomplish this? God gives us practical guidelines to follow in Scripture. "The tongue that soothes is a tree of life; the barbed tongue, a breaker of hearts" (Proverbs 15:4 TJB).

The first step in following these guidelines is deciding to control our tongues. Gentle speech begins with shifting our attitude to purposefully speak instead of saying out loud whatever pops into our brains. Proverbs 21:23 states: "Keep a guard over your lips and tongue and keep yourself out of trouble" (NEB). We realize that we need a filter to check every word that leaves our mouths. Is it gentle? Is it kind? Is it constructive? Is it an arrow or a soothing balm? Is it the word Jesus would speak? "Those who consider themselves religious and yet do not keep a tight rein on their tongues deceive themselves, and their religion is worthless" (James 1:26).

Knowing what not to say is as important as knowing which healing words to use. We practice gentle speech when we

- *Hold our tongue.* Proverbs 10:19; 17:27–28; 30:32.
- *Listen before speaking.* Proverbs 18:13–15; James 1:19–20.
- *Wait to speak at the right time.* How often have we said the needed words at the wrong time? Proverbs 25:11; Ecclesiastes 3:7.
- *Use soothing words to calm tempers instead of inciting conflict.* Proverbs 15:1; 25:15.
- *Speak encouraging words to benefit the listener as our Lord does.* Ephesians 4:29; 2 Thessalonians 2:16–17.
- *Speak with honesty.* Psalms 15:2; Proverbs 16:13; 24:26.
- *Speak graciously.* Proverbs 22:11; 31:26.
- *Speak with kindness.* Proverbs 10:32; 12:25; 16:24.
- *Speak the truth in love.* Ephesians 4:15; 1 Corinthians 13:1.
- *Share constructive wisdom and life-giving knowledge.* Proverbs 10:11; 10:31; 15:2; 18:21.

Throughout Proverbs, the practical book of the Bible about relationships, wise speech is contrasted with foolish speech. You may know people who pride themselves on sharing truth and biblical wisdom with everyone around them. But when they do this without listening first, knowing when not to speak, patiently waiting for the best time to speak, and only choosing words that are soothing, encouraging, gracious, and kind, the results are often hurtful and build walls in relationships. The best intentions can do more harm than good. So how do we realistically speak truth with gentleness into a hurting world?

SPEAKING TRUTH WITH GENTLENESS AND LOVE

Courage is what it takes to stand up and speak; courage is also what it takes to sit down and listen.

—Winston Churchill

If we follow the scriptural guidelines to be tender, kind, humble, and patient; and if we hold our tongue and only speak gentle words, then how do we represent God's truth in the world? How do we speak up for what is right while saying no to evil? How do we not appear weak, fearful, and passive?

We are called to defend the helpless, and we do not want to turn a blind eye to injustice. We realize that we need to speak the truth in love, but how do we accomplish this challenging task in our daily reality?

You need not wrestle with this dilemma alone. Scripture offers practical advice on how to pour love and truth, blended together, into the lives of people around you, from your closest family members to strangers and acquaintances who are hostile to our Christian faith and values. As with other facets of the Spirit, this discipline of speaking the truth with love and gentleness requires self-control, hard work, and practice.

You may feel better when you explode on the scene, boldly speaking truth and taking action. But those words are ineffective if directed at people who are not listening. Do they feel better after your lecture or sermon? We may be quick to "shake the dust off our feet and leave" or "not cast our pearls before swine" when we meet with opposition (Matthew 7:6; 10:14). We are often too quick to discount people who do not welcome our beliefs, telling ourselves, "Well, I did my part. I am not responsible if they reject God."

You are not responsible for people's responses to God, but you are responsible for how you gently open ears to listen and how you present God's extended healing hand. James 2:12–13 tells us that our words and actions should be covered in mercy. Scripture teaches that Jesus calls us to invest in cultivating loving relationships that encourage people to listen to us and observe us. This process of nurturing genuine friendship as Jesus did requires time. We must earn the right to be heard. But first we must look inward, not outward.

Make me preach Thee without preaching— not by words, but by my example.

—John Henry Newman

SAYING NO BEGINS WITH US

Be gentle to all and stern with yourself.

—Saint Teresa of Avila

God calls us to focus on our own behavior and brokenness. He tells us to not judge others and to take the plank out of our own eye before we focus on the speck in our brother's eye (Matthew 7:1–5). Throughout Scripture, God makes it clear that He is the sole judge of humanity. Remember that we are only fellow patients recovering in the hospital.

Saying a firm no begins with speaking to ourselves. Kaitlyn, whom you read about in chapter 9, said a gentle but firm no to men who invited her to have sex with them, and she credited her behavior to years of spiritual muscle memory. She did not judge these men or give them a lecture about biblical abstinence. She simply said no to herself first. If men pressed her to know why she declined, then she was honest in explaining her reasons and her faith. You can imagine the interesting turn those conversations took. A few men did want to know more about this life-changing experience with Jesus.

Female peers of Kaitlyn scoffed at her decision more often than men did. When women pressed Kaitlyn to explain why she followed antiquated religious rules, she found ways to discuss that God is the champion of women's rights and His guidelines in Scripture are intended to keep women safe, protecting them from pain and regret. Kaitlyn practiced saying a "gentle, exemplary no" without arguing, judging, or lecturing. She graciously explained her reasons when asked, which led to engaged conversations and deepened relationships. She sometimes listened as women shared their own painful experiences with failed affairs, adoptions, abortions, or broken relationships.

One pastor told me that holding to Christian convictions is no reason to be impolite. When people offer him an alcoholic drink or cigarette, he tries to graciously respond, "No, thank you. But thanks for offering." He realizes that people are sharing a kindness and offering a gift to him. They are extending the hand of friendship. He wants to pursue the relationship.

The world is watching when we say no to engaging in an unethical or illegal act at work, refuse to indulge in an extramarital affair, maintain our temper, avoid becoming drunk, reject escaping with drugs, or refuse to succumb to a host of other temptations. Our example of saying yes to Christ and no to the world's fleeting pleasures speaks volumes. Yet how we say no is just as important.

Before he was crucified, Jesus prayed to his Father for His disciples: "My prayer is not that you take them out of the world but that you protect them from the evil one. They are not of the world, even as I am not of it. Sanctify them by the truth; your word is truth. As you sent me into the world, I have sent them into the world" (John 17:15–18).

Jesus has sent us into the world, not beside the world or in front of the world. We live in the thick of the world. God does not remove us from this world; He protects us as we journey through it. He sanctifies us with His truth and Word.

EARNING THE RIGHT TO BE HEARD

> When we learn how to speak and what to say, how to articulate our theology, how to translate our theory, we must earn the right to say it—through the practices of silence, patience, and presence. Only one who has learned to be silent is prepared to speak.
>
> —David Augsburger

Our boldest words are spoken through our behavior. Perhaps you are familiar with this popular saying: "You may be the only Bible that somebody reads." Our biblical goal is to be above reproach. People will be more open to listening to us when they observe these characteristics:

WE LISTEN TO THEM FIRST

To answer a question before you have heard it out is both stupid and insulting. A man's spirit may sustain him in sickness, but if the spirit is wounded, who can mend it? Knowledge comes to the discerning mind; the wise ear listens to get knowledge.

Proverbs 18:13–15 NEB

David Augsburger writes that "silence is the language of respect" and people have a profound need to be heard by a "listener who will be silent enough to practice the hospitality of listening."[2] The hospitality of listening invites a conversation. Before we speak, we need to check that first we have listened to God and second we have listened to our invited "guest." We come with no agenda. True silent listening requires us to give our guest's words our undivided attention and respect, not simply think about what we will say when there is a break in conversation.

WE LIVE A CONSISTENT EXAMPLE OF CHRISTLIKE BEHAVIOR

In everything set them an example by doing what is good. In your teaching show integrity, seriousness and soundness of speech that cannot be condemned, so that those who oppose you may be ashamed because they have nothing bad to say about us.

Titus 2:7–8

Wives, in the same way be submissive to your own husbands so that, if any of them do not believe the word, they may be won over without words by the behavior of their wives, when they see the purity and reverence of your lives.

1 Peter 3:1–2

In the Titus 2 passage, Paul shows Titus how to mentor young men, especially those who oppose his teachings, by setting a good example, having integrity, and choosing wise speech. In 1 Peter 3:1-2, Peter tells wives of unbelieving husbands that the most powerful way they can communicate the gospel is through practicing godly behavior without speaking words. In 1 Peter 3:15-16, Peter calls us to explain our faith (when asked) to the world with gentleness and respect and to behave as Christ would.

Allow this important anchor of practicing gentleness to fully sink in. Whether we are interacting with our closest family members, young people we are mentoring, acquaintances, or friends, our Christlike behavior is the key to communicating God's truth. Unless we live the example, our words will fall on deaf ears. And often our example can be so influential that words would only get in the way.

"Wives, in the same way be submissive to your husbands." When Peter encourages wives to hold their tongues and let their behavior speak for them, most people inside and outside the church automatically associate the word "submission" with pathetic weakness. Yet Jesus submitted to his Father's will unto death. Peter's advice is applicable to most close relationships, especially our closest family relationships. If we cannot practice Christ's gentleness, kindness, and restraint with those closest to us who know us best and see our truest selves, then we are fooling ourselves. Perhaps we now realize the strength required to practice our Lord's gentleness and restrain critical, harsh words.

God is not calling us to the weakest actions; He is calling us to the most effective actions.

We are prepared to answer everyone with gentleness and respect
Always be prepared to give an answer to everyone who asks you to give the reason for the hope that you have. But do this with gentleness and respect, keeping a clear conscience, so that those who speak maliciously against your good behavior in Christ may be ashamed of their slander.

1 Peter 3:15–16

Preach the Word; be prepared in season and out of season; correct, rebuke and encourage—with great patience and careful instruction.

2 Timothy 4:2

We must be prepared. Scripture is telling us, "Don't wing this. Don't just react. It's too important." We need to put careful time and thought into preparing gentle and respectful words when sharing our faith and values. We want to take great care in patiently sharing God's truth. More important is understanding that we are preparing an answer. Our words are offered in response to a question. People are listening when they are asking questions and seeking our input. Our behavior, in complete contrast to the world's self-preserving behavior, should intrigue them. Perhaps they see that we fully trust God through life's most painful obstacles and want to know, "Why?"

We tailor our words for our audience

The righteous man can suit his words to the occasion; the wicked know only subversive talk.

Proverbs 10:32 NEB

Be wise in the way you act toward outsiders; make the most of every opportunity. Let your conversation be always full of grace, seasoned with salt, so that you may know how to answer everyone.

Colossians 4:5–6

In addition to being prepared, Scripture also calls us to know our audience. How we wisely share God's truth depends on the person we are speaking with. We need to listen to people to learn about them. We need to develop relationships and know people well before we are ready to answer their questions.

We are called to make the most of every opportunity and interaction with this recipe for conversation: May our words overflow with grace and be seasoned with salt. Our words should immerse the listener in a soothing bath of the miraculous love and limitless grace of Jesus Christ. In biblical times, salt was used as a seasoning, a preservative to keep food from rotting, and a disinfectant for cleaning wounds. Matthew 5:13 tells us that we are the salt of the earth. When we eat a meal that is seasoned to perfection, not too much or too little, we desire to keep eating those delicious flavors. When we season our conversation with the same care, the listener should long to hear more healing words. We are the seasoning, not the main meal, and should not be tasteless or overpowering.

When asked to speak, we offer loving counsel not judgmental criticism

> Anyone who speaks against a brother or sister, or judges them, speaks against the law and judges it. When you judge the law, you are not keeping it, but sitting in judgment on it. There is only one Lawgiver and Judge, the one who is able to save and destroy. But you—who are you to judge your neighbor?
>
> James 4:11–12

> The words of a man's mouth are a gushing torrent, but deep is the water in the well of wisdom.
>
> Proverbs 18:4 NEB

> Counsel in another's heart is like deep water, but a discerning man will draw it up.
>
> Proverbs 20:5 NEB

Criticism can poison any relationship. Toxic criticism and implied judgment are the gushing torrent of words from a man's mouth. Wise counsel is wisdom drawn up from the well. The listener draws up the refreshing water and seeks it out. The listener asks for counsel.

We want to be available to graciously share God's truth and wisdom when it is requested and wanted. The people I know that have the healthiest relationships live by these rules:

- Never give unrequested advice and listen more than you talk.
- There is only one eternal Judge, and you are not it.

We answer kindly no matter how difficult our situation is

To this very hour we go hungry and thirsty, we are in rags, we are brutally treated, we are homeless. We work hard with our own hands. When we are cursed, we bless; when we are persecuted, we endure it; when we are slandered, we answer kindly.

1 Corinthians 4:11–13

Our test lies not in answering kindly with gentleness when life is going well and our problems are few. Our test lies in answering kindly when life is filled with pain. People are watching how we respond. Imagine that you are in Paul's situation. You are hungry, thirsty, wearing ripped clothing, homeless, required to work hard, brutally treated, cursed, persecuted, and slandered. Would you feel like answering kindly and blessing your persecutors? Most of us would lash out with angry, hurtful words.

BALANCE: A TIME AND PLACE

Injustice is what shows up when love is absent from the heart.

—Mark Labberton

There is definitely a time and place for Christians to speak out boldly and take swift action—when people's lives are in danger, when the downtrodden are abused, when children are starving or abandoned, when the elderly are mistreated, when the helpless are oppressed, when women in war zones are raped, when young people are enslaved, or any time or place evil runs rampant in our world.

If you want to be immersed in one of the best examples of walking the fine line between embodying gentle Christlike behavior and speaking out against evil, read Eric Metaxas' biography about Dietrich Bonhoeffer. Through Metaxas' masterful words, you will experience Bonhoeffer's journey that led him to speak out against Hitler when many German pastors remained silent, and you'll also read about his participation in the failed assassination plot of Hitler. Bonhoeffer, like other pastors and fellow Christians, was imprisoned and executed for opposing Hitler. Throughout the ordeal, Bonhoeffer extended kindness to everyone in his path, from fellow believers to SS guards, without sacrificing his unwavering commitment to obey Jesus Christ.

Throughout this chapter you have read Paul's frequent advice to speak with gentleness and respect—to "answer kindly." Yet throughout the book of Acts, Luke writes about Paul speaking out boldly and inciting sharp disputes. Paul often caused an uproar when he spoke. His fellow Christians were not spared these disagreements. He had such a serious argument with Barnabas that they parted ways and pursued different directions in their ministries (Acts 15:36–41).

Similar to Jesus, Paul directed his harshest words at the religious establishment, not at unbelieving Gentiles. Lest we dismiss this target audience, let us remember that the people who most closely approximate the Pharisees today are severe, judgmental Christians who prize rules and dogma above mercy.

Note how this dispute described in Acts 23 exploded. The dispute became so violent that the commander was afraid Paul would be torn to pieces by them. He ordered the troops to go down and take him away from them by force and bring him to the barracks. The following night the Lord stood near Paul and said, "Take courage! As you have testified about me in Jerusalem, so you must also testify in Rome" (Acts 23:10–11).

Then Paul became a hunted man.

> The next morning some Jews formed a conspiracy and bound themselves with an oath not to eat or drink until they had killed Paul. More than forty men were involved in this plot.
>
> Acts 23:12–13

Paul's words made them so furious that they were intent on murdering him. I doubt the conspirators interpreted Paul's words as soothing and gentle. In contrast Paul spent other seasons of his life remaining in one place as seekers came to him.

> [Paul] took the disciples with him and had discussions daily in the lecture hall of Tyrannus. This went on for two years, so that all the Jews and Greeks who lived in the province of Asia heard the word of the Lord.
>
> Acts 19:9–10

> For two whole years Paul stayed there in his own rented house and welcomed all who came to see him. He proclaimed the kingdom of God and taught about the Lord Jesus Christ—with all boldness and without hindrance.
>
> Acts 28:30–31

Scripture shows us that human, imperfect Paul struggled to find the balance between speaking truth with gentleness, love, and respect and boldly preaching about his Lord. He offers his scriptural advice out of his own deficiency. God used him in different ways in changing seasons of life.

OUR BEST EXAMPLE: JESUS' CALM WORDS

Then Jesus was led by the Spirit into the desert to be tempted by the devil. After fasting forty days and nights, he was hungry. The tempter came to him and said, "If you are the Son of God, tell these stones to become bread." Jesus answered, "It is written: 'Man does not live on bread alone, but on every word that comes from the mouth of God.' "

Matthew 4:1–4

During the temptation of Christ (Matthew 4:1–11), we observe that Jesus was starving when the master tempter began to harass and test him. Jesus must have felt the same weakness and desperation that we experience when we reach our lowest point and are most vulnerable to the enemy. Jesus answered him by reciting God's Word from Deuteronomy and Psalms. His final words were, "Away from me, Satan! For it is written: 'Worship the Lord your God, and serve him only.' "

Jesus was calm yet firm when speaking to the enemy of our souls or the religious establishment that rejected Him. Our Lord carefully chose His words.

The teachers of the law and the Pharisees brought in a woman caught in adultery. They made her stand before the group and said to Jesus, "Teacher, this woman was caught in the act of adultery. In the Law Moses commanded us to stone such women. Now what do you say?" They were using this question as a trap, in order to have a basis for accusing Him. But Jesus bent down and started to write on the ground with his finger. When they kept on questioning him, he straightened up and said to them, "Let any one of you who is without sin be the first to throw a stone at her." Again he stooped down and wrote on the ground. At this, those who heard began to go away one at a time, the older ones first, until only Jesus was left, with the woman still standing there.

John 8:3–9

This passage is my favorite example of how Jesus quietly but firmly communicated truth while using few words. Wouldn't we love to know what Jesus wrote on the ground? Both times? We can imagine that He was listing the sins of the woman's accusers. He didn't become angry or raise His voice. Jesus didn't argue with them. He did not incite an uproar. He calmly communicated truth, truth that protected the adulterous woman. Then Jesus told her: "Has no one condemned you? . . . Then neither do I condemn you. . . . Go now and leave your life of sin" (John 8:10–11).

Respected religious leaders did not converse with adulterous women or anyone who would contaminate them. One of their main complaints against Jesus was that he did associate with "sinners." Jesus embraced hurting people. He listened to them. He engaged them in deep conversation. He was genuinely interested and asked them questions about their lives, certainly not because He didn't already know the answers. He was honest yet gracious. He spoke to them with gentleness, kindness, and respect, and He seasoned his wise and healing words to perfection.

We know, our Father, that we are praying most when we are saying least.

—Peter Marshall

O Word Made Flesh, stand at the gate of my mouth. Be my voice this day that the words I speak will be healing, affirming, true, and gentle. Give me wisdom to think before I speak. Bless the words in me that are waiting to be spoken. Live and abide in my words so that others will feel safe in my presence. Surprise me with words that have come from you. Oh, place my words in the kiln of your heart that they may be enduring and strong, tempered and seasoned with love and resilience. Give me a well-trained tongue that has been borne out of silent listening in the sanctuary of my heart. May my words become love in the lives of others.

—Macrina Wiederkehr

PERSONAL RETREAT

- Read Ephesians 4:31–32. Can exploding with bitterness, rage, anger, and slander coexist with practicing compassion and forgiveness?

- Do you agree with Mark Labberton's statement that "Words can tear our heart out"? Proverbs 15:4 describes a barbed tongue as the breaker of hearts. Why are words so powerful? Why are thoughtless, careless words as damaging as purposefully cruel words?

- Read some of the noted verses and create a mental checklist of what is not godly speech and what is godly speech. Mull over a recent significant conversation. Did your godly speech habits outweigh your ungodly habits or vice versa?

- Why is listening and holding our tongue critical to effective communication and "speaking as God speaks"? Do your words tend to soothe and heal or provoke and open wounds?

- Do you agree with the advice of Saint Teresa of Avila: "Be gentle to all and stern with yourself"? When have you communicated God's truth to others by saying no to yourself and being a Christlike example instead of judging or preaching?

- Think about your significant relationships with unbelievers as well as fellow believers. What communication habits do you practice that earn you the right to be heard?

- In conversations about Scripture, are you careful to differentiate between clear biblical truth and your opinions about interpreting biblical passages? This requires humility. Even Paul explained to listeners the difference between his opinions and God's truth. Read 1 Corinthians 7:10–12 as an example. Keep in mind, however, that Paul's words were inspired nonetheless.

- Do you identify more with Paul in the midst of his disputes or Jesus' calm conviction in the midst of conflicts?

- What is your balance between "answering kindly" and standing up to injustice and evil? Would you have risked everything to speak out against Adolf Hitler? Would you have participated in the assassination plot on his life?

If you are going to work for the cure of souls, you cannot choose the kind of souls you are going to work with.

—Oswald Chambers

Giving more than receiving is the best way to work on a soul.

—Thomas Moore

Currently Christianity is known for being unlike Jesus; one of the best ways to shift that perception would be to esteem and serve outsiders. This means being compassionate, softhearted, and kind to people who are different from us, even hostile toward us.

—David Kinnaman

PRACTICING GENTLE KINDNESS

He has showed you, O man, what is good; and what does the LORD require of you but to do justice, and to love kindness, and to walk humbly with your God?

Micah 6:8 RSV

*M*icah 6:8 has become a popular verse and rallying cry for Christians who seek justice for the oppressed, yet I believe this verse equally calls us to love kindness and practice it with humility. We follow a God who extends loving kindness and tenderness: "In your loving kindness, answer me, Yahweh, in your great tenderness turn to me" (Psalm 69:16 TJB). In the King James translation of the Psalms, God's tender love is called His *lovingkindness*. Our response to Him should be to literally love kindness.

For ten chapters you have been reading about practicing gentle restraint and self-control. We restrain our strength and quiet our souls to practice tender gentleness. We restrain our pride and impatience to practice humility and patience. We restrain thoughtless words to practice gentle communication. So you may be thinking that mirroring Christ calls you to be a quiet, serious, and carefully controlled person. Not the life of the party, right? Not someone who makes a friend laugh uncontrollably or relishes fun, crazy ideas, and surprises? To be honest, this dull, restrained person sounds like someone that we would respect for admirable behavior but have no desire to hang out with on a regular basis.

But people from all walks of life loved hanging out with Jesus. He was magnetic. People went to great lengths to steal a glimpse of Jesus, touch Him, listen to Him speak, or converse with Him. Whatever piece of us resembles Jesus should draw people to us like a magnet. Scripture teaches that Jesus is the face of God's kindness (Ephesians 2:7; Titus 3:4). If our commitment to Jesus drives people away, then something is seriously wrong.

Restraining actions and words that would hurt people is where our calling begins, but this is only one side of the spiritual equation. The other side of the equation is the opposite of restraint. We are called to be lavish with kindness, love, forgiveness, laughter, and joy. We are called to be generous with all our resources of knowledge, time, money, talents, and gifts. First, we minimize any damage that our carelessness can cause so we can maximize pouring God's love into people's lives. Think of our mission as surprising people with God's overwhelming goodness.

You may remember reading in chapter one that Stanley Horton finds *kindness* to be the best translation of *gentleness* in our current English language. He writes, "Gentleness is a kindness and generosity that tries to put people in the best light."[1] Generosity is the tangible outpouring of kindness. The *New Oxford American Dictionary* defines *kindness* as "the quality of being generous, considerate, and friendly." It defines *generous* as "showing kindness and giving more than expected." Think of generosity as extravagant kindness. The point is that we may intend to be kind but our intent is worthless if we do not back that up with tangible action.

Can we practice gentle kindness without practicing generosity to the needy? Proverbs teaches that they are one and the same act:

The kindly man will be blessed, for he shares his food with the poor.

Proverbs 22:9 NEB

The man who is kind to the poor lends to Yahweh: he will repay him for what he has done.

Proverbs 19:17 TJB

To oppress the poor is to insult his creator, to be kind to the needy is to honor him.

Proverbs 14:31 TJB

When we are kind to the needy, we honor God. When we withhold kindness, we insult God.

EXTRAVAGANT KINDNESS

He who pursues virtue and kindness shall find life and honor too.

Proverbs 21:21 TJB

Jesus was a kind, generous man in daily life, always giving more than expected. When Jesus performed His first miracle, He didn't turn the water into mediocre wine but into the finest wine. When He multiplied loaves and fishes to feed crowds on two separate occasions (totaling nine thousand people), there was plenty of food left over. When Peter asked Jesus, "Lord, how many times shall I forgive my brother when he sins against me? Up to seven times?" Jesus responded, "I tell you, not seven times, but seventy-seven times." Our Lord performed His ultimate act of giving more than we expected or deserved on the cross.

You will remember reading in chapter 10 about the sinful woman of Luke 7:36–50 who poured pure nard, an expensive perfume, on Jesus. She was extravagant with her gift. Theologians may debate whether Jesus was anointed with perfume on two or three occasions, but the message of kindness does not change. When Mary pours the nard on Jesus, the house is filled with the fragrance of the perfume (John 12:3). Judas objected, claiming that the perfume should have been sold and the money given to the poor. Knowing that Judas was a thief, Jesus replied, "Leave her alone. . . . It was intended that she should save this perfume for the day of my burial. You will always have the poor among you, but you will not always have me" (John 12:4–8). Jesus was grateful for the extravagant kindness of his faithful followers.

Ephesians 4:32 tells us to "be kind and compassionate to one another, forgiving each other, just as in Christ God forgave you." We are called to be as extravagant with kindness, compassion, and forgiveness as with tangible gifts.

Tangible Kindness

A man's attraction lies in his kindness, better a poor man than a liar.

Proverbs 19:22 TJB

What does biblical kindness look like? In Acts 28:1–10 we learn that the islanders of Malta showed Paul and the other prisoners "unusual kindness" after their shipwreck. They welcomed them by building a fire in the midst of rainy, cold weather. The chief official of the island welcomed them into his home and entertained them for three days. Paul healed the official's ill father and cured other sick islanders. The islanders honored their visitors and furnished them with needed supplies when they set sail (Acts 28:10). Compare this description of kindness with Jesus' description of the Good Samaritan who finds a man beaten by robbers, stripped of his clothes, and left half dead on the road: "When he saw him, he took pity on him. He went to him and bandaged his wounds, pouring on oil and wine. Then he put the man on his own donkey, took him to an inn and took care of him. The next day he took out two denarii and gave them to the innkeeper. 'Look after him,' he said, 'and when I return, I will reimburse you for any extra expense you may have' " (Luke 10:33–35).

The Good Samaritan takes care of every need the injured man has. Then Jesus tells us to "Go and do likewise." Matthew 25:34–40 tells us that whatever we do to tangibly care for the "least of these" is doing the same for Jesus.

> "Lord, when did we see you hungry and feed you, or thirsty and give you something to drink? When did we see you a stranger and invite you in, or needing clothes and clothe you? When did we see you sick or in prison and go to visit you?" . . . "Truly, I tell you, whatever you did for one of the least of these brothers of mine, you did for me."
> Matthew 25:37–40

These familiar verses remind us that biblical kindness is not theoretical. These tangible offerings are gifts that people can touch, see, feel, and taste. Kindness can appear in the form of a glance (Proverbs 15:30), words (Proverbs 10:32; 16:24), or a variety of gifts. When Peter healed a crippled beggar, he explained it as an "act of kindness" (Acts 4:9). Proverbs 3:27–28 (TJB) advises that we not wait on performing acts of kindness: "Do not refuse a kindness to anyone who begs it, if it is in your power to perform it. Do not say to your neighbor, 'Go away! Come another time! I will give it you tomorrow,' if you can do it now."

In Front of Our Faces

> What good is it, my brothers and sisters, if a man claims to have faith but has no deeds? Can such faith save him?

> Suppose a brother or a sister is without clothes and daily food. If one of you says to them, "Go in peace; keep warm and well fed," but does nothing about his physical needs, what good is it? In the same way, faith by itself, if it is not accompanied by action, is dead.
>
> James 2:14–17

Sharing kindness is not intended to be a detached program. Biblical kindness has no middle man. Examples through Scripture clearly show us that we are called to minister to the people in front of us. They have names and faces. Mark Labberton writes, "If we say we love God and don't love our neighbor, it turns out we don't love God. In other words, our faith is only fiction."[2]

I am inspired by the creative, gentle ways that followers of Jesus extend kindness to those around them. One woman quietly mails checks and gift certificates to families that are financially struggling. Another hands out five-dollar meal gift cards to homeless people she sees on the street. Another family leaves notes of encouragement or appreciation and lavish tips wherever they have been served. One couple who owned an apartment building learned that one of their tenants had lost her job and was diagnosed with cancer. They discounted her rent and wrote a letter to all their friends explaining her plight. Soon the checks started pouring in to help her. I learned of one postman who gave away almost everything he earned to anonymously help people on his route, a deed that was made public only after his death.

The people in one church recognized that their kindness should grow out of their location, situated across the street from their town's middle school. Church staff could have been annoyed that parents were using the church parking lot to drop off and pick up their children. Instead these believers began serving breakfast daily to middle school students, and this became a thriving ministry to the community. Another group of believers realized that their church was on the path that most high schools followed when walking home. They set up tents outside and offered drinks and snacks to students after school. Another church is located downtown in a major city, across the street from a large university. Believers from this body offer regular study sessions with dinner served. This church also sends believers into local inner-city schools to mentor and tutor students, provide needed school supplies, and clean and paint classrooms.

Sharing our time is as valuable as sharing other resources, whether we offer a listening ear to friends in crisis or come alongside to help with mundane tasks. One woman lost her job and did not have money to share with others, so she offered her driving services to elderly people in her neighborhood to take them to medical appointments and transport them on errands. Another unemployed woman provided emergency child care for the children of young mothers. A retired couple has spent years caring for their sick parents who live with them while providing afternoon care for their grandchildren.

One pastor left a comfortable church position in an idyllic suburb to move with his family to a street in the inner-city where drug dealers and prostitutes conducted nightly business. He didn't feel that he could minister to people who needed Jesus without living among them and gaining their trust. When an educator in California, who was also an ordained Baptist minister, became the county school superintendent, he declined his $800,000 salary for three years because he did not want to burden his cash-strapped schools. He believed that helping young people and teachers was his calling.

I believe that ministries similar to these examples are occurring quietly all over our country and world. They are not labeled as "church outreaches." No expectations of the receivers are implied. Believers see an opportunity that God has put directly in front of them and they extravagantly respond. They are living examples of Romans 12:8, which states that if our gift is to contribute to the needs of others, let us give generously. In other words, whatever we do as Christ's representatives in the world, let us do it with extravagance. Don't skimp or cut corners. We are reminded of the destitute widow who approached Elisha for help in 2 Kings 4:1–7. When he asked her what she had in her house, she replied, "Nothing at all, except a flask of olive oil" (NLT). This ordinary staple became the source of God's provision for her. God uses what we already have in our possession and multiples it.

> This is how we know what love is: Jesus Christ laid down his life for us. And we ought to lay down our lives for our brothers and sisters. If anyone has material possessions and sees his brother or sister in need but has no pity on them, how can the love of God be in that person? Dear children, let us not love with words or tongue but with actions and in truth.
>
> 1 John 3:16–18

We are called to extravagantly shower people with gentle kindness. We are told that this is what love looks like. This is faith in action. First Peter 1:22 calls us to love each other deeply, with all our hearts. This overpowering love is the essence of God's miraculous kindness. It is our privilege to lavishly share it.

No influence is so powerful in human society as practicing kindness.

—Peter Ainslie

PERSONAL RETREAT

- In what forms does kindness come? Are Christians called to be lavish? In what ways?

- In Acts 10:4, the angel told Cornelius, "Your prayers and gifts to the poor have come up as a memorial before God." Remember that generous kindness has no middleman. Think of acts of kindness that you have performed in the past months for people that God placed in your path. Who is in front of your face that needs God's tangible touch of lovingkindness?

- When did you perform an extravagant act when you gave more than expected?

- Read 2 Peter 1:5–8. Think about how brotherly kindness follows self-control and patient perseverance, and leads to love. Does this list share similarities with spiritual fruit and the clothing of Christ? Note that practicing these qualities will make us effective and productive in following our Lord.

God loves each of us as if there were only one of us.

—Saint Augustine

We must boldly enter into environments where grace flourishes and does its best work. Christian insulation and a safe life are not what you and I signed up for when we said we would follow Jesus. He was never insulated from people's pain, and he sure didn't keep to safe places. He hung with the not-so-perfect people of the world and showed them what Christianity was all about.

—Mike Foster

BOLD GRACE

Yet the LORD longs to be gracious to you; therefore he will rise up to show you compassion.

Isaiah 30:18

*A*s we come to the end of our scriptural journey together, let us summarize our biblical calling described in this book as graciously treating everyone with the gentleness of Jesus Christ. To mirror our compassionate Father, we want to practice a consistently gentle disposition toward all men (Titus 3:2 NEB) and be kind to everyone (2 Timothy 2:24). Our gentle, peaceful spirit is rooted in receiving and pouring out God's grace and mercy. People who withhold grace and mercy cannot be gentle with others because their well is dry.

Scripture is crystal clear on this point. We are to treat everyone as Christ would. God's Word does not give us the option to choose which Christlike qualities we will practice or the people who should receive gentle treatment. Remember that our calling is easy to understand yet incredibly difficult to practice.

Paul struggled as much as we do to daily imitate his Lord. With much effort, Paul offered courageous gentleness to the world and encouraged followers of Christ to engage in this gentle battle. Let us follow Paul's example to go boldly into places where people desperately need Christ's gentle touch. And let us follow Christ's example to love people with passionate abandon.

I hope you have drawn your own conclusions about our original question, "Is gentleness for wimps?"

God may start with wimps, but then He transforms them into fearless, courageous warriors who bring Christ's love and gentleness to the front lines. The world's weapons are powerless in the face of God's unfailing love. Go engage in the gentle fight of faith.

Every gentle word, every generous thought, every unselfish deed, will become a pillar of eternal beauty in the life to come. We cannot be selfish and unloving in one life and generous and loving in the next. The two lives are too closely blended—one but a continuation of the other.

—Rebecca Springer

NOTES

CHAPTER 1

1. Stanley Horton, "Gentleness—Meekness," Enrichment journal.ag.org (2013): 1.
2. Stanley Horton, *What the Bible Says About the Holy Spirit* (Springfield, MO: Gospel Publishing House, 1976), 179.

CHAPTER 3

1. Philip Yancey, *Grace Notes* (Grand Rapids: Zondervan, 2009), 398.

CHAPTER 4

1. Richard Mouw, *Uncommon Decency: Christian Civility in an Uncivil World* (Downers Grove, IL: InterVarsity Press, 2010), 38.
2. David Kinnaman and Gabe Lyons, *Unchristian* (Grand Rapids: Baker, 2007), 11, 39.
3. Ibid., 24–25.
4. Ibid., 30–31.
5. David Kinnaman, "Are Christians More Like Jesus or More Like the Pharisees?" Barna.org (April 2013): 2–3.
6. Kinnaman and Lyons, *Unchristian*, 228.
7. Antonio Anderson, "Bullets and Beatitudes," *First Things* (May 2013): 20–21.

8. Stanley Horton, *What the Bible Says About the Holy Spirit* (Springfield, MO: Gospel Publishing House, 1976), 178.

CHAPTER 6

1. "'Impatient Nation': Attention Span Loss in U.S.," ABC News, March 1, 2012, http://abcnews.go.com/WNT/video/impatient-nation-attention-span-loss-us-15829715.

2. Thomas à Kempis, *Imitation of Christ*, ed. Harold Chadwick (North Brunswick, NJ: Bridge-Logos, 1999), 22.

3. Philip Yancey, *Grace Notes* (Grand Rapids: Zondervan, 2009), 168.

4. à Kempis, *Imitation of Christ*, 5.

5. Susan Cain, *Quiet: The Power of Introverts in a World That Can't Stop Talking* (New York: Crown, 2012), 197.

6. Ibid., 268.

CHAPTER 10

1. Mark Labberton, *The Dangerous Act of Loving Your Neighbor* (Downers Grove, IL: InterVarsity Press, 2010), 129.

2. David Augsburger, "Silence, Patience, and Presence," *Fuller Theology News and Notes* (Fall 2012): 32.

CHAPTER 11

1. Stanley Horton, *What the Bible Says About the Holy Spirit* (Springfield, MO: Gospel Publishing House, 1976), 179.

2. Mark Labberton, *The Dangerous Act of Loving Your Neighbor* (Downers Grove, IL: InterVarsity Press, 2010), 30.